Van Cleef, *The Quiet Gun* (1957)

LEE VAN CLEEF

BEST OF THE BAD

by Michael G. McGlasson

Lee Van Cleef: Best of the Bad

© 2010 by Michael G. McGlasson

All rights reserved.

No portion of this publication may be reproduced, stored, and/or copied electronically (except for academic use as a source), nor transmitted in any form or by any means without the prior written permission of the publisher and/or author.

Published in the United States of America by:

BearManor Media
1317 Edgewater Dr #110
Orlando FL 32804

bearmanormedia.com

Printed in the United States.

Typesetting and layout by Valerie Thompson

ISBN—978-1-62933-976-4

TABLE OF CONTENTS

ACKNOWLEDGMENTS . . . 1

FOREWORD: "A GOOD GUY, AFTER ALL"
BY MIKE MALLOY . . . 2

INTRODUCTION . . . 6

THE EXTRAORDINARY LIFE OF LEE VAN CLEEF . . . 14

THE MYTHIC ARCHETYPE OF THE VILLAIN . . . 33

THE GUNFIGHTER AND THE BOUNTY HUNTER:
FACT VS. FICTION . . . 39

THE GUNS OF LEE VAN CLEEF . . . 48

PORTRAIT GALLERY . . . 56

THE GUNMEN:
COLONEL DOUGLAS MORTIMER: VENGEANCE IS MINE . . . 61
ANGEL EYES: 200,000 REASONS TO KILL . . . 64
FRANK TALBY: A MAN WITHOUT A CONSCIENCE . . . 66

FADE OUT: THE LEGACY OF LEE VAN CLEEF . . . 71

BIBLIOGRAPHY . . . 77

INDEX . . . 81

Acknowledgments

First of all, the author would like to thank the entities responsible for creating, developing, and distributing the following films on DVD: *Day of Anger*, Wild East Productions, Inc., NY, fully restored widescreen version, 2002, the Spaghetti Western Collection, Volume Three; Metro-Goldwyn-Mayer, *The Good, The Bad, and The Ugly*, 2-Disc Collector's Set, fully restored widescreen version, 2007, and *For a Few Dollars More*, widescreen version, 2005.

In addition, the author would like to thank the following individuals: Mike Malloy, for his gem of a foreword, suggestions, and ardent support for this project; Tom Betts, spaghetti western historian for providing critical biographical information on Lee Van Cleef; Henry C. Smith, Sr., Trustee and Membership Chairman, Somerset County Historical Society; Jim Sommerville, Reference Librarian, Somerville New Jersey Public Library; Sebastian Haselbeck, Executive Editor and founder, the Spaghetti Western Database; David R. Chicoine, proprietor of the Old West Gunsmith website; Christopher Gullo, for permission to quote from Eli Wallach's letter on Lee Van Cleef; and lastly, Lee Van Cleef for all of the pleasure and excitement he brought to the screen for millions worldwide.

Foreword:
"A Good Guy, After All"

Antihero. This word gets thrown around a lot when describing the protagonists occupying the cruel, ruthless world of the Italian-made spaghetti westerns of the 1960s and 1970s, where the only difference between the (alleged) Good Guys and the (extreme) Bad Guys is that the former limits their killings to the latter. So naturally, "antihero" is usually the label bestowed upon the spaghetti western roles of Lee Van Cleef who was easily one of the genre's biggest and most iconic stars. But why then did I become such a Van Cleef diehard, even to the point of becoming his first published biographer, during my teen years? After all, I was raised with such a strong sense of right and wrong that even as late as adolescence, I could barely understand the motivations of a protagonist who wasn't always wearing a spotless white hat.

Maybe then, Van Cleef's spaghetti roles are deceptively heroic, or at least they end up that way. Take for instance his first Italian western, Sergio Leone's *For a Few Dollars More* (1965). In this career-transforming role, Van Cleef plays Colonel Douglas Mortimer, a bounty hunter (generally a cinematic profession ripe for antiheroism) who seems intent on greedily collecting the rewards on the heads of a vicious gang of outlaws, even aiding in lawbreaking to do so. Teamed up with Manco, a younger bounty hunter played by Clint Eastwood, Mortimer eventually abandons the idea of collecting the rewards and focuses instead on bringing his sister's killer to justice—while letting all the reward money go to his younger partner.

This trajectory of a Van Cleef character evolving into a hero right before our eyes—that is, at some point during a film's running time—became a formula that was used in most of his best spaghettis (except for his villainous turns in *The Good, the Bad, and the Ugly* and *Day of Anger*). This "deceptive and ultimately heroic" characterization was used most purely in *Death Rides a Horse* (1967). Any review of this film will tell you that Van Cleef's character is a former bandit seeking payoffs from his erstwhile gang members for wrongfully pinning a crime on him. Oh sure, this is an adequate description of the character as the film begins, though as the story progresses, he becomes increasingly sympathetic, even paternal, toward a young man who's been trailing the same gang for murdering his family. In the end, Van Cleef's character abandons his self-interested quest for payback and instead aids the young man in finding closure to his situation.

The often comedic spaghetti western *Beyond The Law* (1968) offers much the same "redemption arc" for Van Cleef's character as he again transforms from a greedy bandit to an unqualified hero (and in this one, there is further change from a goofball to a stoic tough guy). Even when Van Cleef plays a peace officer in a spaghetti western, sometimes he's not a bona fide hero until the end as proven by *The Big Gundown* (1966). In this film, his lawman character is neither corrupted by nor abusive of his authority; instead, his less-than-heroic status is derived from his naiveté about law and order and its even-handed application to all classes (because while a worldly innocence may be an endearing quality in some cases, it's not particularly heroic). A couple of early scenes—one involving a barber, the other a desperate widow—uncharacteristically depict Van Cleef's lawman as either a wisecracker or cold-hearted, and they only muddy the transition. But by the film's end, he basically evolves into a full-blown hero who remains every bit committed to justice but now approaches "justice" with a realistic wariness.

A follow-up was made to *The Big Gundown*, but sadly, Van Cleef's character was nowhere to be found. It would have been interesting to have seen what this Van Cleef spaghetti western character would've done post-transformation, operating on pure heroism. Fortunately, we have *The Grand Duel* (1972) for something similar. The entire *Grand Duel* story occurs with Van Cleef's character acting bravely and with much self-sacrifice to help save a wrongfully accused man running for his life. He does not need to transform during the course of the film because he already did so prior to the story's point of attack (through all of the rogues we meet along the way in the film, we learn that Van Cleef's character used to be rather different). And in a fake-out introduction intended to play on our expectations about the dog-eat-dog spaghetti landscape, his character is presented to us as yet another uncaring, mercenary bounty hunter when in fact he is just going undercover as such. This is my favorite on-screen performance of the man, possibly because he is so stalwart throughout.

So, Lee Van Cleef a spaghetti western antihero? Sure, at some points, but these characters were often moving toward something better, and that fact often gets overlooked via the general mean-spiritedness of the genre. And what is more, Van Cleef depicts heroism with such a perfect world-weariness that he never comes off as a stuffy, straight-laced, goody two shoes protagonist.

I'm not sure whether Michael McGlasson, the author of *Lee Van Cleef: Best of the Bad*, agrees with my appraisals of the above roles. Although I've read much of his book, I haven't at the time of this writing delved into his interpretations of these characters. But I think the book is big enough to encompass any conflicting opinions since it strives to be more than a mere entertainment biography. With unexpected chapters like "The Guns of Lee Van Cleef" and "The Gunfighter and the Bounty Hunter: Fact vs. Fiction," *Lee Van Cleef: Best of the Bad* achieves the status of being a fun pop-culture book (although one that's solidly researched) centering around a single actor and his creative spaghetti western output—a book that sometimes gets enjoyably peripheral in its scope.

In any case, there surely is room for all sorts of Van Cleef coverage these days because his cult following continues to grow by leaps and bounds, even as we move beyond the twenty-year anniversary of his premature passing in 1989. It might be a statement of the obvious, but worldwide DVD (both commercial and gray-market discs) and the Internet—two things I didn't have access to while writing *Lee Van Cleef: A Biographical, Film and Television Reference* in 1995—have ensured that new Lee Van Cleef devotees are being created all the time.

His western performances are obviously timeless. I've recently, though, become a bigger fan of *poliziotteschi*, or Italian crime films, the high-action fad that replaced the spaghetti western in the 1970s.

I sometimes catch myself wishing Van Cleef had switched to these crime movies instead of stubbornly sticking with Italian westerns after they fell out of vogue. But then again, his 1970s output would probably seem more dated now, and may not have aged as well.

Also, after the fact of completing my Van Cleef book, I had the opportunity to meet many of the late actor's co-stars, from those who worked with him during his 1950s Hollywood career to his spaghetti western castmates, even some co-stars during his 1980s "denouement." Not a single one of them had an outright negative thing to say about ol' Lee; in fact, so fondly is he remembered that I've even received some gestures of kindness from some of these co-stars, just for my tenuous association of having written a posthumous biography. So, for all of the above reasons, Lee Van Cleef is an anti-non-un-antihero to me, and, yes, that works out to be . . . a hero.

Mike Malloy
July, 2010

INTRODUCTION

My first cinematic encounter with Lee Van Cleef occurred on a hot July afternoon in 1960 at the Shafer Theater, a small movie house run by brothers Martin and Charles Shafer in Garden City, Michigan, some twenty miles from downtown Detroit. Like most so-called movie palaces built in the late 1940s, the Shafer Theater boasted a huge, canopy-like marquee with big colored light bulbs and a narrow wrap-around area below the lights where a lowly usher would stand on a ladder and line up black plastic letters to spell out the fare of the day, usually a double billing of low-budget, black and white monster movies by American International Pictures (AIP) with Sam Arkoff and James Nicholson as founders and producers.

On this particular July afternoon, the black letters on the marquee spelled out IT CONQUERED THE WORLD and just to one side of the front entrance doors near the ticket booth, a one-sheet movie poster in a display case was dominated by a strange-looking monster, shaped like a weird, overgrown turnip with beady eyes, razor-sharp fangs, and a pair of stubby arms ending with two menacing claws. The main protagonist in this 1956 film, directed by schlockmeister of the B-movies Roger Corman, was none other than Lee Van Cleef in the role of Dr. Tom Anderson, a typical 1950s paranoid scientist who befriends the above-mentioned turnip which turns out to be an alien from the planet Venus bent on "conquering the world" by forcing humans into submission through devious mind control.

At this time, I was not at all familiar with Lee Van Cleef as a film actor, but once inside the theater and perhaps by the middle of the second reel, I came to realize that I had seen him many times on TV in series like *The Untouchables* as Frank Diamond, *Lawman* as Deputy Clyde Wilson, and *Bonanza*, one of the longest-running westerns in the history of American television. There was also something about his face that I found quite appealing because it was different than most male movie actors with only a hint of typical Hollywood handsomeness.

Not surprisingly, Van Cleef's face has been described in many ways over the years—hawk-like with steely eyes and accented with a demonic smile; imbued with the pure essence of malevolence; utterly wicked and sinister, plus a whole range of other interpretations. Sergio Leone who provided Van Cleef with his big acting break in *For a Few Dollars More* once remarked that he "had a face resembling a falcon,"[1] but it is Van Cleef's eyes that have garnered the most attention. He allegedly once remarked, "Being born with a pair of beady eyes was the best thing that ever happened to me,"[2] and it is rumored that he had one green eye and one blue eye, but according to his US Navy enlistment records for 1942, his eye color is described as brown.

Fast forward to 1969 and the Algiers Drive-In, owned and operated by the Shafer brothers, which also boasted a beautiful marquee with a large, green neon palm tree and those black plastic letters lined up along the base. Opened to the public in 1956 with a 120 foot-long screen, the Algiers showed a limited number of first-run feature films, mostly aimed at families, and many re-released gems from the early to mid 1960s and a few monster B-movies from the 1950s. It was here that Lee Van Cleef came back into my life in the guise of Colonel Douglas Mortimer in *For a Few Dollars More* with Clint Eastwood reprising his earlier role as the laconic and ambiguous "Man With No Name."

With the help of this often extremely violent film, Van Cleef firmly established his stature as an iconic film actor which made it possible for him to become one of the most widely-recognized (but under-appreciated) screen villains of all time, comparable to Vincent Price, Bela Lugosi, Boris Karloff, Neville Brand (Al Capone in *The Untouchables* TV series), Richard Widmark (Tommy Udo, *Kiss of Death*, 1947), Jack Palance (Jack Wilson, *Shane*, 1952), Richard Boone (Cicero Grimes, *Hombre*, 1967), and even Henry Fonda in his portrayal of the utterly ruthless, psychopathic Frank in Sergio

Leone's 1968 masterpiece *Once Upon a Time in the West*.

In cinematic terms, a true villain must exhibit certain traits of personality in line with traditional literary archetypes, such as an overwhelming proclivity for wickedness, selfishness bordering on numbing conceit, and a desire for absolute power and control over others. Physically, villains are sometimes quite attractive if not downright sexy or, as in most instances, they may be rather ordinary-looking with a whisper of repulsiveness. But most importantly, villains must be complex characters with evil intentions.

After seeing *For a Few Dollars More* at the Algiers Drive-In in 1969, I began a personal quest to discover more films featuring Lee Van Cleef in the role of the western "bad guy." One source that proved to be helpful was the *Detroit Free Press* with its cheaply-printed movie advertisements plastered on the last few pages of the sports section and just before the comics. To my great delight, there were many spaghetti westerns to be found here, films that were generally produced in Italy and shot in Spain between 1961 and 1977 with budgets hovering around $250,000, an amount that today would hardly cover the fee for a second-rate Hollywood actor.

Some of the best included Sergio Corbucci's *Django* (1966) which helped to establish the revenge motive in Eurowesterns while increasing the level of gratuitous violence to new and bloody heights; *A Pistol for Ringo* (1965), directed by Duccio Tessari[3] with Montgomery Wood as Ringo, a character clearly modeled after Eastwood's "Man With No Name" (a.k.a. Joe) in *A Fistful of Dollars* (1964); and Franco Giraldi's *A Minute to Pray, A Second to Die* (1968), starring Alex Cord as a young gunslinger haunted by his violent past which he suddenly recalls with the pealing of church bells.

There also happened to be several films that I was not familiar with prior to 1969, such as Sergio Sollima's *The Big Gundown* (1966) with Van Cleef as Jonathan Corbett, a bounty hunter out to capture Cuchillo (Tomas Millian) wanted for rape; Giulio Petroni's[4] *Death Rides a Horse* (1967) with Van Cleef as Ryan, an intelligent and crafty bandit just released from prison and seeking revenge against his former partners in crime; and the superb *Day of Anger* (1967), directed by Tonino Valerii[5] with Van Cleef as Frank Talby, an aging gunfighter without any morally redeeming human values who attempts to take control of the town of Clifton with the assistance of young and inexperienced Scott Mary, played brilliantly by Giuliano Gemma (a.k.a. Montgomery Wood). With the exception of Angel Eyes in *The Good, The Bad, and The Ugly*, Van Cleef's portrayal of Frank Talby stands as the penultimate western "badman," due to his brutality, self-centeredness, and the fact that ice water truly does flow through his veins.

One day, I chanced upon another movie advertisement that took up half a page, but this time it was in full color with a nice black border. In the upper right-hand corner, there stood three men—Clint Eastwood on the left, Eli Wallach on the right, and Lee Van Cleef in the middle, with the bottom displaying a Civil War battle scene, guns blazing, Union soldiers screaming and running amid chaos and violence. In the upper left-hand corner, a caption in blood-red letters said, "For Three Men, the Civil War Wasn't Hell. It Was Practice!" Produced in 1966 but not released in the United States until 1968 by United Artists, *The Good, The Bad, and The Ugly* was the third and final installment of Sergio Leone's "Man With No Name" trilogy which many agree re-stylized and re-invented the genre of the American western.

After its US debut, film critics and historians quickly became interested in this spectacular film because of its directing, cinematography, production values, and the artistic renderings of character, political/social themes, motifs, and iconography. One area which they unfortunately seemed to have neglected is the film's historical accuracy via its scenery, costumes, sets, war imagery, and weaponry. As Daniel Edwards relates, Sergio Leone went to extraordinary lengths to make his Spanish scenic locations "look as much like the American-Mexican geographical region (southern New Mexico, Arizona, and northern Mexico) as possible;" however, as a result of Leone's use of expansive, widescreen vistas, the landscape in *The Good, The Bad, and The Ugly* exudes "a slightly alien feel which creates a setting that appears to be European yet does not look American either."[6] Nonetheless, Van Cleef's character of Angel Eyes (a.k.a. Setenza) seems well at home amid this Euro-alien diorama with its vast deserts, wide open plains, towering mountains, and rural towns which Leone reproduced with astonishing accuracy.

Since those long ago nights at the Algiers Drive-In, my fascination with the life and career of Lee Van Cleef has not waned; in fact, as a result of the availability of Eurowesterns on VHS and DVD, this interest has greatly expanded, so much so that I decided after giving it much thought to start on a new journey into uncharted territory, much like Van Cleef's character of Colonel Mortimer in *For a Few Dollars More* who abandons his privileged life as the "best shot in the Carolinas" and heads for the open expanses of the Old West in search of adventure, fortune, self-discovery, and revenge.

It should also be admitted that as a writer with a deep appreciation for American/European literary cinema and the actors and actresses, directors, cinematographers, set designers, and other personnel who made it all possible, I was somewhat dumbfounded to learn that the life and film career of Lee Van Cleef had been almost entirely neglected by film historians and scholars except for a thin collection of magazine and newspaper articles, interviews, and a few shallow extrapolations on his roles in American and European productions, beginning with his performance as Jack Colby in Fred Zinnemann's *High Noon* (1952) and ending around the early 1980s with John Carpenter's *Escape From New York* and the TV series *The Master*.

Exactly why Van Cleef has been overlooked is quite puzzling, but it is obvious that because of his decision to work primarily in Europe between 1965 and the mid 1980s, his position as an American film actor suffered, much unlike that of Clint Eastwood whose career exploded after *The Good, The Bad, and The Ugly* and upon returning to Hollywood in the late 1960s as a legitimate film star. It is interesting to note that when Van Cleef died at the age of sixty-four, many American newspapers decided not to run his obituary because they felt he was not a major Hollywood celebrity worthy of coverage.

But things were different in Europe, where Van Cleef's death was considered as a major event, due in part to his status as one of the top-ten biggest box office draws in the history of late twentieth-century European cinema. According to Tom Jennings, Van Cleef's longtime agent, "I think he could have been a greater movie star, as big as Charles Bronson or Clint Eastwood, if he had come back from Europe sooner than he did. He liked working abroad and was always a bigger star everywhere else than in Hollywood."[7]

But today, some twenty years after his death, Lee Van Cleef is a true cinematic icon and is much appreciated (if not idolized) by a wide audience of spaghetti western enthusiasts who see him as a figurehead of the Eurowestern tradition. A quick search on the Internet will reveal a number of well-organized websites devoted to Van Cleef and Sergio Leone, along with references to anything even remotely connected to the sub-genre. There are also several excellent books that should be required reading, such as Robert C. Cumbow's *The Films of Sergio Leone* (1990), and Christopher Frayling's *Sergio Leone: Once Upon a Time in Italy* (2008), jam-packed with beautiful poster reproductions and supported by a well-written text.

Book-wise, there is only one important work devoted to Van Cleef's acting career currently available—Mike Malloy's *Lee Van Cleef: A Biographical, Film and Television Reference* (McFarland, 1998, re-issued 2005). In this exhaustive work, Malloy provides film-by-film details on cast and credits, a plot synopsis for each film/TV appearance, and a short overview on Van Cleef's roles. Also included is an in-depth discussion on the ABC network series *The Master* with Van Cleef as John Peter McAllister, an aging ninja master who reluctantly agrees to teach a young, inexperienced pupil how to survive in a world filled with violence.[8]

In a November 2009 interview, Malloy admits that in order to write Van Cleef's biography, he was forced to ransack used bookstores, video shops, and libraries close to home where he often spent days searching through reels of microfilm. At some point during this ransacking, Malloy came into contact with "Turkish spaghetti fanatic" Cenk Kiral ("A Fistful of Leone" website) and was then put in touch with Western historian Tom Betts who gladly provided additional research materials. Unfortunately, Malloy's writing process for the book was nearing its end, thus making what Betts had provided somewhat redundant. However, Malloy did manage to "slip in a few additions"[9] concerning Van Cleef's biography. Adding to the problem was that Van Cleef's immediate family members were quite reluctant to grant interviews to those interested in revealing new facets about the life of "old Angel Eyes."

Unlike Malloy's book which covers every Van Cleef film and TV appearance spanning more than thirty-five years, *Lee Van Cleef: Best of the Bad* focuses on three specific classics—Sergio Leone's *For a Few Dollars More* and *The Good, The Bad, and The Ugly*, and Tonino Valerii's *Day of Anger*. These films have been chosen because they represent Van Cleef's best screen performances within the sub-genre of Eurowesterns and illustrates his ability to bring a scripted character to full human embodiment. To make everything perfectly clear, *Best of the Bad* devotes three sections to the characters portrayed by Van Cleef in these films as if they are living human beings with positive and negative traits. In addition, the plotlines of these films are exceptional as compared to most spaghetti westerns that came out of Italy during the 1960s.

It should be mentioned that the epithet "Best of the Bad" as found in the title of this book implies two meanings. First, it refers to the ultimate "badness" of an individual character, such as Angel Eyes and Frank Talby; and second, a character like Colonel Douglas Mortimer does indeed possess "bad" but also "good" traits, a type of duality or doubling. In other words, a "bad" character can express "the best" of human qualities like compassion, forgiveness, and friendship. But in the end, it all comes down to motivation, for all characters, whether "good" or "bad," are driven by goals and objectives and a sense of duty to either help others less fortunate than themselves or to utterly destroy them.

ENDNOTES

1. Sergio Leone on Lee Van Cleef. *Spaghetti Cinema*. Internet. May 4, 2009.
2. Lee Van Cleef Biography. Internet Movie Database, 2010.
3. Tessari was also responsible for co-writing the screenplay for *A Fistful of Dollars*.
4. Ironically, during the writing of this introduction, Petroni passed away at the age of 92; on April 28, Furio Scarpelli, co-writer of *The Good, The Bad, and The Ugly*, also died at the age of 90.
5. Valerii served as the assistant director for Leone's *For a Few Dollars More*.
6. Sergio Leone. *Senses of Cinema*. Internet. 2002.
7. Actor Lee Van Cleef, 64; Played Villains. Associated Press Release obit. December 18, 1989.
8. *The Master* was canceled after thirteen episodes, running between January 20 and August 31, 1984.
9. Lee Van Cleef Forum. Internet. November 7, 2009.

THE EXTRAORDINARY LIFE OF LEE VAN CLEEF

"First lesson: Never beg another man."
Frank Talby, *Day of Anger*

After reviewing dozens of biographies on the Internet, some highly-detailed and others slipshod and filled with inaccuracies, it appears that Lee Van Cleef never had to "beg another man" for anything during his rather short life. Born on January 9, 1925 in the small farming community of Somerville, New Jersey, Clarence Leroy Van Cleef, Jr., descended from the Dutch settlers of New Amsterdam in the 1600s, discovered early on that he had a penchant for the outdoors. "I went on my first canoe trip," he says, "when I was two years old. My dad and mother took me up the Raritan River, and there I was, squatting in the middle of a canoe. I can still remember that."[1] Part of this love for the outdoors involved going to camp, hunting and fishing, and excelling at swimming and archery; a natural extension was joining the Boy Scouts and becoming a Star Scout, two ranks below an Eagle. Some of his indoor activities included playing the piano and the trombone, a reflection of his lifelong interest in the study of music which might have come about through his mother, Marion Van Fleet, allegedly at one time a professional singer.

As a young man, Van Cleef also possessed a deep appreciation for reading and was especially interested in folklore, poetry, and the occult. In his high school yearbook for 1942, alongside his picture, he included a quote from Charles Godfrey Leland (1824 to 1903), a well-known American scholar, folklorist, and author of dozens of books on a wide range of topics, such as witches and witchcraft, Etruscan/Roman/Egyptian magic, English gypsy sorcery, music, and even a pamphlet on Paracelsus, a sixteenth-century alchemist. "My heart is full of longing/For the secrets of the sea," wrote Leland,

"And the heart of the great ocean/Sends a thrilling pulse through me." Taken from *The Gypsies*, published in 1882, this quote symbolizes Van Cleef's desire to escape from the drudgery of Somerville as a delivery boy for a downtown grocery store in the late 1930s and his yearning to experience the "secrets of the sea" as an able-bodied US sailor.

In June of 1942, at the age of seventeen, Van Cleef graduated from Somerville High School and almost immediately enlisted in the United States Navy. Since he was a minor, his father, Clarence Leroy Van Cleef, Sr., had to consent to his son's enlistment, as well as verify his true age with a birth certificate issued by the Board of Health in Somerville. It is at this time only ten months after the attack on Pearl Harbor by the Japanese that Lee Van Cleef's life went on a tangent, taking him into a world filled with adventure, travel, and extreme danger, much like millions of other young American men eager to serve their country overseas in the theaters of Europe and Asia during a conflagration known as World War II.

On October 16, 1942, Van Cleef enlisted in the US Navy at the Naval PHI Little Creek Base in Norfolk, Virginia, as the first graduating senior from Somerville High School to enter the armed forces. According to the *Somerville Gazette*, Lee's father had served in the "Great War" as a sergeant in the First Infantry in France and returned to the states in July of 1919 when he became an assistant cashier at the Second National Bank of Somerville.[2] At a pay rate of $50 a month, Van Cleef went into the service as an able-bodied, apprentice seaman and was sent to the Naval Training Station in Newport, Rhode Island, for basic training. His physical characteristics at this time are described as six feet tall[3] and 170 pounds, with brown eyes, brown hair, and a ruddy complexion.

On November 27, 1942 after spending less than six weeks in basic training, Van Cleef ended up at the Fleet Sound School in Key West, Florida, and achieved the rate of sonarman third-class after graduating on January 2, 1943. Less than five weeks later, he was admitted to the US Naval Hospital in Brooklyn, New York, with a severe case of scarlet fever which in some cases can result in rheumatic fever, an inflammatory disorder that can damage the valves of the heart. This is possibly linked to his later heart problems which plagued him most of his adult life. After being treated, he was discharged from the hospital on February 15, 1943 and then transferred to the US Naval Hospital in St. Albans, New York, for further treatment.

Van Cleef's first assignment occurred on March 15, 1943 upon being transferred to New York City for duty aboard the USS SC 681, a submarine chaser built by the Thomas Knutson Shipbuilding Corporation of Long Island in late 1942 and commissioned for service on March 8, 1943,[4] thus making it a brand-new vessel and ready to sail off into the wide Atlantic in search of German submarines or U-boats. Like most third-class sonarmen, some of his duties aboard ship included sound and radar watches, operating sonar sound gear, standing lookout on the bridge, and monitoring controls in the sonar compartment to maintain operating efficiency. His service aboard this vessel lasted until early January of 1944 and his rate changed from third-class to second-class seaman. On January 16, he was transferred to the Fleet Sound School in Key West, Florida, for a refresher course in sonar operation where he ranked number one in a class of twenty-two with a grade of eighty-two percent.

Seven weeks later, Van Cleef was transferred to the Minecraft Training Center in Little Creek, Virginia, where he underwent extensive training until April 4, 1944. Upon completion, he was sent to the Receiving Station in Savannah, Georgia, to await new orders. Two weeks later, he received a new assignment to the USS *Incredible* (AM 249), a 530 ton first-class minesweeper built by the Savannah Machine and Foundry Company in early 1943 and commissioned in April of 1944. Like the USS SC 681, this was also a new vessel and was equipped to handle almost any type of warfare on the high seas with a .50 caliber machine gun, two Bofors 40 mm. anti-aircraft cannon, a Hedgehog anti-submarine mortar launcher, and numerous depth charges.

Once aboard the USS *Incredible*, homeported in Norfolk, Virginia, in mid April of 1944, Van Cleef achieved the rank of sonarman first-class and quickly found himself as a participant in the invasion of southern France between August 15 and October 17, 1944, known as Operation Dragoon.[5] Van Cleef excelled while performing his ship-board duties as a sonarman and during minesweeping operations off the coast of Menton, France. His commanding officer commended him for "calmly and efficiently performing your duties while under heavy shellfire from enemy shore batteries" and while under attack by "approximately twelve human torpedoes to such an end that this vessel was able to engage both shore batteries and human torpedoes with heavy return fire," thus resulting in "a successful operation."[6]

While serving aboard the USS *Incredible* in the Mediterranean Sea in December of 1944, Lee Van Cleef demonstrated his bravery (or perhaps foolhardiness) and moral character when he dove thirty feet from the bridge of the ship and into the icy-cold water to save the life of a spaniel puppy named Rusty, the ship's mascot, that had been washed overboard in heavy seas. As he relates in a letter to his parents:

Rusty was out on the fantail and a wave came along, washing her overboard. We had to get permission to break formation and go back for her. That took about fifteen minutes until we finally found her. I was up on the bridge smoking my pipe. Well, I shed the knife I had on and my shoes and yelled up for permission to go after her, so I dove off the bridge. When I hit the water, I heard something snap in my mouth. That happened to be my pipe stem. I don't know how my teeth escaped from breaking. Luck, I call it. However, I got Rusty all right. She was swimming to beat everything. Quite a current, too. They threw us a life ring and pulled us aboard.

The next day after this harrowing incident, Rusty ran up to Van Cleef and curled around his legs. "I guess that swim," he says, "was worth my favorite pipe."[7]

In January of 1945, the USS *Incredible* was sent on a special mission to Russia and the Black Sea to perform minesweeping activities as part of the Crimean Conference, a strategic meeting in Yalta held on February 11, 1945 and attended by British Prime Minister Winston Churchill, President Franklin Delano Roosevelt, and Soviet leader Joseph Stalin to plan for the final defeat and disarmament of Nazi Germany and how to partition Europe between the Allies. The USS *Incredible* also served as a rescue patrol vessel in the Black Sea and was one of six escort ships assigned to President Roosevelt's special convoy. After completing its mission in mid February, the USS *Incredible* was ordered to Palermo, Sicily.

In May of 1945, the USS *Incredible* returned to Norfolk for repairs in dry dock and then proceeded to the Pacific Ocean in late July, steaming straight through the Panama Canal towards Pearl

Harbor. Fortunately, Van Cleef and his crewmates did not end up in battle, due to the unconditional surrender of the Japanese Empire to the Allies in mid August. Instead, they were sent to the East China Sea to clear away mines in the area of the Ryukyu Islands southwest of Japan. This assignment was also successful, and the USS *Incredible* returned to the states on February 17, 1946, and docked in San Pedro, California. As a side note, on January 29, 1945 after crossing the International Dateline, Van Cleef was fully initiated into the Order of the Golden Dragon via a brutal initiation ritual which during World War II might have included the use of the "Devil's Tongue," an electrified piece of metal poked into certain places on the bodies of "pollywogs" or non-initiated sailors and new recruits. Van Cleef also had a ship's anchor tattooed on his lower right forearm.

In effect, this brought Van Cleef's naval career to a fine conclusion. During his three and a half years in the US Navy, he accomplished a great deal and changed from an inexperienced young man into a respected and honored combat veteran. Also, his "ruddy complexion" was gone, replaced by hard lines and rugged features which he would use to his advantage in the years to come. Prior to his discharge on March 6, 1946 in Toledo, Ohio, Van Cleef was made eligible by the commanding officer of the USS *Incredible* to wear seven decorations—the Asiatic-Pacific medal and War Campaign ribbon, the African-European-Middle East medal (a bronze star for meritorious service), the American Area medal, the Good Conduct medal, and the World War II Victory medal and ribbon.

Van Cleef was now free to return to Somerville, New Jersey, to be with his wife Patsy Ruth whom he had married on December 10, 1943 and once again take up the life of a low-wage laborer, toiling day after day on a farm somewhere in Hunterdon County, helping out with the plowing, planting, cultivation, and harvesting of grains and vegetables, feeding livestock, milking cows, and running a tractor. During his spare time at home, he might even play the trombone or the piano, and then call it a night and retire to bed, worn out but ready to face another grueling day on the farm.

At some point, Van Cleef worked at a hunting and fishing lodge in Maine, but soon realized that the pay was not enough to support his wife, son, and daughter. This led to accepting a job as a time study and motions analysts, a technical position that involves increasing the efficiency of a mechanical device. Such a position requires the use of higher mathematics which Van Cleef could have learned during his studies at the Fleet Sound School. Also, circa late 1946, he started his own accounting business, but this too failed to produce a steady income.

But then, sometime around 1948, a strange and "incredible" thing happened to Lee Van Cleef. One day, a co-worker from the time study plant suggested that they take a trip to Clinton, New Jersey, located on the banks of the Raritan River and not too far from Somerville, to try out for a role in Clinton's small theatre district set in the countryside, known as the Clinton Music Hall Players. This co-worker just happened to be a member of the Music Hall Players and must have seen something in his friend that sparked his imagination. Here was the beginning of the acting career of Lee Van Cleef. According to an October, 1979 interview in William R. Horner's *Bad at the Bijou*, Van Cleef's first acting role was in Thornton Wilder's acclaimed *Our Town* as George Gibbs, one of the play's main protagonists, an innocent and sensitive, all-American schoolboy who expects to inherit his uncle's farm at some point in his life. As shown by his response in this interview, Van Cleef was astonished, to say the least—"I tried out for the part and damn, if I didn't make it!"[8]

His second acting role and his first as a leading man was in an amateur production of Harry Segall's *Heaven Can Wait* as boxer Joe Pendleton, the same character played by Warren Beatty in the 1978 film version but as a quarterback. Obviously, Van Cleef made quite an impression on the right individuals, for not long after appearing in this play, the director took him to New York City, the world's theatre capital and home to Broadway, where he met talent agent Maynard Morris of the MCA Agency which in the early 1950s represented movie giants like Tyrone Power, Gene Tierney and Gregory Peck.[9] One suggestion made by this director was that Van Cleef should take up the study of dramatics; however, the idea of becoming a full-fledged, professional actor had never occurred to him.

Nonetheless, Van Cleef ended up at the Alvin Theatre on 52nd Street, now known as the Neil Simon Theatre, and was hired for a minor role as an MP (military policeman) in *Mister Roberts*, based on Thomas Heggen's 1946 novel about his experiences aboard the cargo ship USS *Virgo* (AKA-20) in the South Pacific during World War II. This acting job was in a national touring company and was first auditioned in New York City and once on the road for fifteen long months, Henry Fonda joined the company as Lieutenant JG Roberts which he reprised in the 1955 film version.[10]

Mr. Roberts was originally performed at the Alvin Theatre on February 18, 1948 with Joshua Logan[11] as director and co-writer and ended its run on January 6, 1951 which is a good indication of when Van Cleef was on the road touring America. Ironically, the original 1948 cast of the New York-based *Mr. Roberts* included Eli Wallach as Stefanowski, a lowly deckhand; also, sometime around late 1945 after appearing in a failed Broadway show and searching for new work, Wallach found himself in the office of Maynard Morris.[12]

As to his acting style, Van Cleef admits that the Shakespearean style, forever linked to stage greats like Laurence Olivier, John Gielgud, and Ralph Richardson, never much appealed to him and that contrary to rumor, he never attended any kind of acting school or academy and instead opted for private lessons. In addition, the "method acting" style, practiced by Marlon Brando, Montgomery Clift, and James Dean, was for him unattractive and non-dimensional. "As far as I'm concerned," says Van Cleef, "method acting confuses audiences more than it tells them anything . . . It's good for some actors, but not for me." However, in order to make his characters more believable and realistic, he often changed his lines of dialogue to complement his natural speech patterns but never altered the basic idea behind the lines. "Sometimes," he says, "I even dropped lines . . . I'd rather just use my eyes, use my face. I always try to find some extra dimension to every character, a sympathetic area."[13]

In early 1951, Van Cleef received a telegram from producer Stanley Kramer, who at the time was looking to cast several roles in his upcoming *High Noon* with Gary Cooper as Marshal Will Kane. Kramer most probably saw Van Cleef in *Mr. Roberts* at the famous Biltmore Theatre in downtown Los Angeles, a longtime major venue for Broadway shows "on the road" which led Kramer to call Van Cleef for an interview which resulted in the role of Jack Colby, a member of the Frank Miller gang. As the story goes, Van Cleef was originally offered the role of Deputy Marshal Harvey Pell which ended up going to Lloyd Bridges, due to Kramer asking Van Cleef if he would have his nose fixed. "I told him to go fuck himself" was his reply to Kramer.[14] Of course, Van Cleef must have assumed that he had no future as an actor in *High Noon*; however, Kramer did call back and gave him the role of Colby.

Without a doubt, it was *High Noon* that gave Van Cleef the opportunity to become one of the greatest screen villains of all time, despite not having any dialogue; it also allowed him to demonstrate his natural abilities to be moody, irascible, sullen, and defiant, all of which he transposed to later films roles as the proverbial "heavy." As Van Cleef puts it, when playing the "heavy" or the antagonist, he often went to great lengths to ensure that his characters were not invincible, that they remained flesh and blood human beings with fatal flaws. "You want to see a guy down on his knees," he says, "crying for mercy," a reference to his role as Alfonso Parral, a half-breed outlaw, in Henry King's *The Bravados* (1958), a tale of revenge and redemption with Gregory Peck as Jim Douglas who mistakenly believes Parral assisted in the rape and murder of his wife. In the film, Van Cleef is shown a picture of Peck's wife in a pocket watch. "I swore I didn't know anything about it. He didn't believe me and plugged me right in the head. Shot me dead away."[15]

One area of Van Cleef's off-screen life that deserves some discussion is his relationship with alcohol. It has been said that creative people, whether writers, painters, musicians, or film/stage actors, are predisposed to drug and alcohol abuse via a psychological connection between creativity and artistic integrity. In some respects, the use of alcohol does elevate the ability to use creative insight and may serve as a "route to mystical transport,"[16] similar in many ways to Van Cleef's idea that an actor must be able to project himself into another dimension to bring his characters to life.

Drinking may also be used as a way to personally experience "the extremes of the human condition" by living in squalor, sleeping in the gutter, and drinking to excess and can symbolize "the exquisite sensibilities" of the artist.[17] After all, Van Cleef was much more than an actor, for he was also a painter of landscapes, seascapes, and the nude female figure, played the guitar, composed and sang his own songs in the style of Johnny Cash and even wrote scenarios and screenplays. As he once remarked, while waiting for movie roles to come his way, he had many other things to do "to keep the creative juices flowing, and I'm not talking about beer and alcohol!" [18]

On the flip side, the belief that drinking is an integral part of the creative process and should be done on a daily basis as a "normal" part of life can lead to serious personal consequences. Although there is no hard evidence that Van Cleef felt this way about drinking, he does give some indication that alcohol was a big problem in his personal life. When speaking of his "lean times" between late 1958 and the birth of the Italian Eurowestern, circa 1964, Van Cleef confesses that "The only regret I've got is the unhealthiness that can come out of idleness," [19] or that drinking to excess while lying around the house solves nothing and only leads to more problems.

In mid October of 1958, Van Cleef was involved in a serious auto accident that resulted in a compound fracture to his left arm and the shattering of his left knee cap during a drive back home in Apple Valley, California, after finishing up on location shooting for *Ride Lonesome*, directed by Budd Boetticher with cowboy hero Randolph Scott. This accident allegedly involved alcohol, meaning that either Van Cleef or the driver of the truck that slammed into him head-on by crossing the center line was driving under the influence. Luckily, Van Cleef survived this terrible accident which demolished his convertible, but the destruction of his left knee cap brought him much pain for the rest of his life, not to mention the steel rod in his left arm. In a 1977 interview with the *Montreal Gazette*, Van Cleef was asked if driving under the influence was partially responsible for this accident. His reply, "Not that time," is practically an admission that he drove while intoxicated on earlier occasions. [20]

Meanwhile, rumors were floating around that he might never ride a horse again, but when sufficiently recovered after two weeks in the hospital, he once again climbed in the saddle. It was possibly just after this accident that Van Cleef slowed down on his drinking so he could devote his creative talents to more profitable enterprises like painting and composing music at his home studio. However, there is strong evidence that he continued to drink quite heavily between the time of this accident and the early 1980s, due to signing a personal check made out for $100 to a liquor store in Tarzana, California, dated February 3, 1982.[21]

There are also the comments made by Luciano Vincenzoni during an interview in April of 1998 with Cenk Kiral, a writer and fanatical admirer of Sergio Leone's "Man With No Name" trilogy. Vincenzoni, the screenwriter for *Death Rides A Horse, For a Few Dollars More, The Good, The Bad, and The Ugly*, and a personal companion to Leone, debunks one of the myths linked to Van Cleef concerning how he first encountered the great Italian director around late 1964 in Los Angeles while searching for an actor to portray Colonel Mortimer in *For a Few Dollars More*.

According to Vincenzoni, while sitting in a bar with producer and assistant director Ottavio Oppo, Leone saw Van Cleef, wearing a black raincoat and hat, walk in or perhaps stumble in, "totally drunk" and ask the bartender for a whiskey. Leone then caught a glimpse of Van Cleef's profile and recognized him almost instantly from *High Noon*. When Leone attempted to strike up a conversation, Van Cleef "thought Leone was teasing him" because "in the last five years, he never worked," due to being an alcoholic. But when Van Cleef's agent showed up after a phone call, Leone signed him for nine weeks of work at a salary of $1000 per week.[22] Vincenzoni also relates that after the success of *The Good, The Bad, and The Ugly*, Van Cleef was able to buy a villa in the San Fernando Valley. "I went to visit him at his beautiful villa . . . and what was amazing is that in the living room there was an enormous bar full of bottles." However, Vincenzoni makes it clear that Van Cleef's drinking never caused any problems on the set, nor did it interfere with his ability to give a more than satisfactory performance.[23]

In mid 1959, during the release of Boetticher's *Ride Lonesome*, Van Cleef made a public appearance at a Western-themed amusement park called Wild West City in Netcong, New Jersey, not too far from Somerville. Since only five or six months had passed since his near-fatal car accident, Van Cleef must have been in much pain, particularly with his knee injury. However, this did not stop him from also appearing at the Cort Theater in downtown Somerville, where a huge crowd greeted him with a banner strung across the theater's marquee—"Welcome! Lee Van Cleef."

After divorcing his first wife in early 1960, Van Cleef was allegedly doing some type of construction to his studio (one rumor suggests it was a playhouse or doll's house for his daughter) and accidentally cut off the third (top) joint of his right-hand middle finger. In *The Good, The Bad, and The Ugly*, this injury is clearly visible during the final scene at Sad Hill Cemetery with Angel Eyes, Blondie, and Tuco facing each other in a final gundown for $200,000 in gold. One could assume that Sergio Leone, being the artistic genius that he was, found this particular injury interesting and used it as a visual cue for the wickedness of Angel Eyes and as a symbol for his violent life as a paid mercenary and bounty killer.

Whether Van Cleef was intoxicated at the time of this injury is not known, but there are some recollections about his drinking by co-stars, colleagues, and close friends dated right around 1960. One of these is provided by actor John Mitchum (1919 to 2001), the younger brother of Hollywood icon Robert Mitchum and best-known for his roles in the first three "Dirty Harry" films with Clint Eastwood. In his aptly-titled autobiography *Them Ornery Mitchum Boys*, published in 1988, Mitchum reveals that one day on a sound stage in Hollywood, Van Cleef invited him into his dressing room for a drink. "I looked around and saw no bottle," says Mitchum, and from a flight bag, Van Cleef produced "a beautiful silver flask. . . It was filled with vodka—but not for long."[24] The friendship between Mitchum and Van Cleef was apparently long-lasting and began in 1955 when they appeared in *The Big Combo*, a cops and robbers thriller directed by Joseph H. Lewis. Van Cleef appeared in only two films between 1962 and 1964, the legendary John Ford's *The Man Who Shot Liberty Valance*, starring John Wayne and James Stewart, and *How The West Was Won*, also directed by Ford. After fulfilling his acting duties in these excellent American westerns with Stewart given full credit for single-handedly gunning down the notorious Mr. Valance (Lee Marvin), and Spencer Tracy narrating how the white man conquered the Far West through Manifest Destiny, Van Cleef once again entered into a prolonged "dry spell," spending almost all of his time as secondary characters in popular TV shows like *Perry Mason, Have Gun Will Travel, 77 Sunset Strip*, and especially *Rawhide* for two episodes, ironically working alongside Clint Eastwood as Rowdy Yates.

At the age of forty in 1965 and after appearing in at least fifty full-length feature films, ranging from straight dramas to cops and robbers, action-adventure, hospital melodramas, and westerns, Lee Van Cleef, thanks to the coincidental meeting with Sergio Leone in that Los Angeles bar, was no longer broke and could now pay his household bills and expenses. He also would not be forced to work as a lowly supporting actor in roles that sometimes went uncredited, such as in *How The West Was Won* as a sleazy river pirate attempting to lure mountain man James Stewart into a cave to rob and kill him and leave his bones to the bears.

Van Cleef's own detailed description on how his life immediately altered after being hired to appear as Colonel Mortimer in *For a Few Dollars More* is quite engaging if not outright surrealistic:

Leone came to Los Angeles and we had a meeting. Late the next night (April 10, 1965), we signed a contract that was thirty percent higher than anything I'd made before. Then his production manager opened an attaché case with thousands in greenbacks. I shelled out ten percent to my agent and went home. I hadn't told my wife Joan about the meeting. I just walked in and threw her the envelope and the rubber band broke and there were greenbacks all over the room. She was between laughing and crying. It took her four times to count it all.

Van Cleef's wife (his second marriage from 1960 to 1974) must have certainly been stunned to see almost $10,000 in cash strewn about the room. The rest of his description is truly heart-wrenching:

You see, the day before was our wedding anniversary and I couldn't give her anything. We just kissed and wished each other a happy anniversary. We were living on TV residuals and unemployment checks and what Joan made as a secretary at IBM. I didn't even have the money to pay the phone bill.[25]

With this in mind, it is astounding that Van Cleef was seriously thinking about giving up acting to pursue another type of career or to become more involved in his painting efforts as a means of income not long before all of this cash fell into his lap. Thus, when Sergio Leone stepped into the life of Lee Van Cleef, his universe changed forever, ushering in a new phase in his acting career that would sustain him for the next twenty years. As Luciano Vincenzoni relates, Van Cleef "made around $10 million in six years" while in Italy between 1965 and the early 1970s,[26] all because of Leone, a true non-conformist who transformed traditional Hollywood western mythology into a completely new sub-genre, overflowing with non-stereotypical characters drawn from a nightmare of violence and degradation.

In the view of Daniel Edwards, Leone portrayed the American West as a place "stripped of all its rhetoric beyond that of burning self-interest and murderous individualism"[27] as compared to classic American westerns produced in the 1940s and 1950s with John Wayne, Randolph Scott, and Charleston Heston. The only American director that even comes close to Leone's visceral representation of the Old West is Sam Peckinpah, the "auteur" of *The Wild Bunch* (1969), a bloody spectacle of greed, bullets, and heavy gratuitous violence.

When the time arrived to begin shooting *For a Few Dollars More* in late April, 1965, Van Cleef must have felt as if he was trapped in a time warp, for he was once again in a place of great natural beauty set amid the rugged coastlines of the Mediterranean Sea where he had served aboard the USS *Incredible*. Here in the province of Almeria in southeastern Spain, just south of the famous Tabernas desert, the location for numerous Hollywood westerns during the 1950s, Van Cleef gave a bravura performance as Colonel Douglas Mortimer, a man seeking vengeance against El Indio (Gian Maria Volonte) for the brutal rape of his sister many years earlier.

As a bounty hunter, Mortimer is shrewd, calculating, and deadly accurate with a weapon; he is also reserved with the bearing of a true Southern gentleman raised to appreciate a firm moral center. In many ways, Van Cleef was like Colonel Mortimer, for he once pointed out "Never hurt a dog. I don't kick dogs,"[28] which harkens back to Rusty the spaniel puppy, washed overboard into the cold sea and then rescued by a brave young man without first considering his own mortality.

Following his highly successful appearance in *For a Few Dollars More*, Van Cleef was offered another important role in the last film of the "Man With No Name" trilogy, a role that sealed his fate as a screen villain and catapulted him almost overnight to international stardom. This of course was Angel Eyes, perhaps the most cold-blooded, unprincipled, and vile character ever to appear in a western film, the ultimate "Best of the Bad" with a heart pounding to the rhythm of all-consuming greed. It would not be stretching the truth too much to say that *The Good, The Bad, and The Ugly* is the Mount Everest of spaghetti westerns, due to embracing many important literary/cinematic traits, such as complex characters, a well-written script, historically accurate sets, costumes, and props, dedicated acting, and a fitting musical score, in this instance by the prolific Ennio Morricone.

While standing victorious in the shadow of *The Good, The Bad, and The Ugly* in late 1966, another phase in the life of Lee Van Cleef began as the lead actor in a series of Eurowesterns, or as he puts it, "I starred on my own instead of with Clint Eastwood. Going to the airport, getting on a plane, jumping . . . to one place or the other. I kept an apartment in Rome for awhile at one point when those pictures were coming fast and furious."[29]

The first was *The Big Gundown* which he made back-to-back with *The Good, The Bad, and The Ugly*; then, within a nine-year period, *Day of Anger* and *Death Rides A Horse* (both in 1967); *Beyond the Law* (1968, Giorgio Stegani); *Sabata* (1969, Gianfranco Parolini); *Captain Apache* (1971, Alexander Singer); *Return of Sabata* (1971), the third film in Parolini's *Sabata* trilogy; *The Grand Duel* (1972, Giancarlo Santi); *Bad Man's River* (1972, Eugenio Martin); *The Stranger and the Gunfighter* (1974, Antonio Margheriti); and *God's Gun* (1976, Giancarlo Parolini). Besides *Captain Apache*, *Bad Man's River*, and *The Stranger and the Gunfighter*, these films represent the finest work by the most experienced Italian filmmakers of the spaghetti western era and are now considered as classics of the Eurowestern tradition.

By 1976, the acting career of Lee Van Cleef had started to decline, partly because the era of the Eurowestern was slowly sinking into the sunset and the fact that his overall health was deteriorating, due to continuing heart problems and a prolonged habit of smoking a pipe which went back to his days in the US Navy and perhaps even earlier as a young man in Somerville. In his 1979 interview with William R. Horner, Van Cleef emphasizes "I am an actor. I enjoy what I'm doing and want to continue doing it . . . I'll never quit until I'm dead,"[30] a prophetic statement which turned out to be quite accurate. Exactly how much damage had been inflicted on his health because of his drinking can only be guessed, but after more than thirty years of consuming hard liquor and beer, going back probably as far as his early navy days, the toll was undoubtedly high.

At the time of this interview, Van Cleef had completed *The Squeeze* (1978, Antonio Margheriti); *The Octagon* (1980, Eric Karson); and John Carpenter's *Escape From New York* (1981), featuring Kurt Russell as "Snake" Plissken. Between 1982 and late 1983, Van Cleef took a break from acting, no doubt because of his failing health and the constant pain related to his knee injury some twenty-three years earlier. There is also reliable evidence that in early 1981, he turned to acupuncture as a way of relieving his pain. Whether this type of exotic treatment was ever of any help is not known.[31]

But beginning in 1984, Van Cleef somehow managed to make seven more films—*Goma-2* (1984, Jose Antonio de la Loma); *Code Name: Wild Geese* (1984, Antonio Margheriti) with Klaus Kinski, the hunchbacked outlaw in *For a Few Dollars More*; *Jungle Raiders* (a.k.a. *Captain Yankee*, 1985, Giovanni Simonelli); *Armed Response* (1986, Fred Olen Ray), with the late David Carradine; *The Commander* (1988, Antonio Margheriti); *Speed Zone* (1989, Jim Drake); and *Thieves of Fortune* (1990, Michael MacCarthy), his final film appearance.

On December 16, 1989, while living at his spacious home at 19471 Rosita Street in Tarzana, California, Lee Van Cleef collapsed and was rushed to St. John's Regional Medical Center in Oxnard, where he died from an acute myocardial infarction. However, the actual cause of his death was due to malignant carcinoma of the epiglottis, a flap of tissue at the base of the tongue that prevents food from entering the trachea or windpipe during swallowing.

This cancerous growth, most probably a result of years of smoking, was diagnosed through a procedure known as a panendoscopy, normally used to examine the lining of the esophagus, only two days before his death. In other words, Van Cleef was unaware that he had this deadly form of throat cancer. He was also diagnosed in April of 1988 as suffering from congestive cardiomyopathy or blockage in the heart which inevitably led to his heart attack.[32] One additional note is that according to Ventura County coroner Craig Stevens, quoted in a *New York Post* obituary, Van Cleef had a permanent pacemaker implanted at an unknown time, but there is no mention of such a device in any of his official death records, one possible reason being that no autopsy was ever performed.

Another area of interest related to this cancer diagnosis dates back to 1956 when Van Cleef appeared in *The Conqueror*, starring John Wayne as Genghis Khan with Susan Hayward and Agnes Moorehead. All of the exterior shots for this film were done near St. George, Utah, some one hundred miles from the famous Nevada nuclear test site, the home of above-ground nuclear weapons testing during the Cold War. Interestingly, the film's director Dick Powell died from cancer in 1963 as did Agnes Moorehead in 1974, Susan Hayward in 1975, and John Wayne in 1979. In total, some ninety individuals linked to *The Conqueror* had either died or been diagnosed with some type of cancer by 1981. Whether Van Cleef's exposure to radiation at this still hot site in 1956 contributed to his death is not known, nor has it ever been proven that the deaths of other personnel associated with this film was linked to radiation exposure.

Lee Van Cleef's funeral took place on December 21, 1989 at the Old North Church in Forest Lawn Memorial Park in the Hollywood Hills. Pallbearers included Rory Calhoun, the star of *The Yellow Tomahawk* and *Dawn at Socorro* (both in 1954) which featured Van Cleef in secondary roles, and the lead actor in *The Colossus of Rhodes* (1961), directed by Sergio Leone; Harry Carey, Jr.; Roy Jensen (*How the West Was Won*, uncredited), and Rance Howard, the father of actor/director Ron Howard, who taught Van Cleef how to properly ride a horse for his role in *High Noon*. One of the honorary bearers was actor Romano Puppo who often performed as Van Cleef's stunt double and appeared in *The Good, The Bad, and The Ugly* as Slim, a member of Angel Eyes' murderous gang.

His final resting place at Forest Lawn, with its well-tended greenery stretching into the distance, is eerily reminiscent of one of Sergio Leone's panoramic views of a sullen, wind-swept plain, dotted here and there with shrubs and patches of grassland. On his bronze gravemarker, a simple epitaph reads BEST OF THE BAD, LOVE AND LIGHT, a fitting reminder that Lee Van Cleef was not only the "Best of the Bad" as a screen villain but also a loving husband

and father, a decorated veteran, and a charismatic human being gifted with the ability to bring light into an otherwise shadowy world.

ENDNOTES

1. Horner, William R. *Bad at the Bijou.* Jefferson, NC: McFarland & Company, 1982, 142.
2. "First High School Student Enlists." October 22, 1942.
3. In his 1979 interview with William R. Horner, Van Cleef states that his height is six-foot, two inches which shows that he matured quite a bit during his service in the US Navy.
4. USS Incredible (AM-249). *Department of the Navy—Naval Historical Center.* Internet, 1999.
5. Ironically, one of the weapons of choice featured in Leone's "Man With No Name" trilogy is similar to the Colt Dragoon .44 caliber, single-action pistol which was used extensively during the Civil War.
6. Human torpedoes were similar to a submarine except for being steered and guided by divers seated on the outside of the vessel. Upon approaching an enemy ship, the divers would release a mine and then ride away on the torpedo.
7. "Sailor Dives Off Ship to Save Pup Washed Into Sea." *Somerville Gazette.* December, 17, 1944.
8. Jefferson, NC: McFarland & Company, 143.
9. Lewis, John. *American Film: A History.* NY: W.W. Norton & Company, 2007, 243.
10. Horner, *Bad at the Bijou*, 144.
11. Logan also directed the 1969 film *Paint Your Wagon* with Clint Eastwood as Pardner.
12. Wallach, Eli. *The Good, The Bad, and Me.* Harcourt & Company, 2005, 92.
13. Horner, *Bad at the Bijou*, 145.
14. Frayling, Christopher. *Once Upon a Time in Italy: The Westerns of Sergio Leone.* New York: Harry N. Abrams, Inc., 2005, 107.
15. Horner, *Bad at the Bijou*, 146.
16. Beveridge, Allan and Graeme Yorston. "I Drink, Therefore I Am: Alcohol and Creativity." *Journal of the Royal Society of Medicine*, 92 (1999): 646.
17. Ibid, 646.

18. Horner, *Bad at the Bijou*, 148.
19. Ibid, 149.
20. "Lee Van Cleef Returns to TV, Villainous Appearance Intact." *Montreal Gazette*. June 6, 1977, p. 34.
21. Personal check signed and dated by Lee Van Cleef (author's collection).
22. Kiral, Cenk. The Good, The Bad, and Luciano Vincenzoni. Internet, 1999.
23. Ibid, Internet.
24. Pacifica, CA: Creatures at Large Press, 180.
25. Morehouse, Rebecca. "Lee Van Cleef Surges to the Top." *Deseret News*. July 20, 1970, p. 43.
26. Ibid, Internet.
27. Sergio Leone. Internet, 2002.
28. Horner, *Bad at the Bijou*, 144.
29. Ibid, 149.
30. Ibid, 149.
31. Signed personal check and dated by Lee Van Cleef, February 2, 1981 (author's collection).
32. Statements by Dr. Stephen Hong, MD, attending physician, taken from his notes attached to Van Cleef's death certificate, December 19, 1989.

The Mythic Archetype of the Villian

"Second lesson: Never trust anyone."
Frank Talby, *Day of Anger*

As film critic Tony Scott observes, the archetypal western film hero is a "complicated figure, and the world he inhabits is a place of flux and contradiction. At the end, the stranger rides off into the wilderness, since the civilization he helped save holds no permanent place for him." In other words, this archetypal western hero exhibits "good" as well as "bad" traits, and the environment in which he lives is filled with uncertainty and opposition. Scott also points out that this archetype is almost always "solitary, self-sufficient, and morally ambiguous—a man of violence with a shadowy background and a haunted look in his eyes."[1]

This is one of the best descriptions of the proverbial cinematic western hero, such as John Wayne, Randolph Scott, Alan Ladd, James Stewart, and dozens of others who brought adventure, conflict and violence to the big screen in America's movie houses, beginning roughly during the late 1940s and into the middle years of the 1960s when the Eurowestern burst onto the scene and forever changed the American western genre.

At first glance, Scott could be speaking of Clint Eastwood as the "Man With No Name," the mysterious stranger who rides into town from nowhere with death trailing behind him like an ominous, lethal plague; there is also *Shane* (1951) with Alan Ladd as the lonely gunfighter trying to forget his past who in the end relents to confront the notorious Jack Wilson (Jack Palance), a "low-down, Yankee liar," in a final barroom showdown. In this sense, the "Man With No Name" and Ladd's Shane are indeed solitary, self-sufficient, and morally ambiguous, sometimes referred to as anti-heroes who possess good and bad qualities but not in equal measure. These antiheroes also usually depart by riding away into the distance, much like Eastwood's *High Plains Drifter* (1973) and *Pale Rider* (1985) whose motivations are at first not at all clear until they face down their adversaries and fill them with lead. Even at this point, the stranger's true motivation often remains vague and obscure, and at the conclusion, usually victorious, he leaves the viewing audience without any adequate closure.

In addition, Scott refers to the "haunted look" lingering in the eyes of the stranger, much like those of Eastwood's Blondie in *The Good, The Bad, and The Ugly* and the bounty killer Manco, Spanish for "one-handed," in *For a Few Dollars More*. In some ways, this haunted look is a reflection of the stranger's past and acts like a window into his soul. However, this window is not transparent; it is opaque like a thick screen and does not allow light to easily pass through it. This is similar to the proverbial well—deep, dark, and mysterious, a bottomless pit filled with dank water that plummets into the unknown.

In contrast, instead of being a hero/antihero, the cinematic western archetype is frequently a villain, a man that cannot be trusted under any circumstances, a man like Frank Talby in *Day of Anger* who warns Scott Mary to "Never trust anyone" after robbing him of his hard-earned money and slapping him to the ground. In literature, the villain plays the role of the antagonist, the enemy and/or opponent of the protagonist, the lead character or hero. As to story structure, the villain often moves the plot forward and makes it possible for the protagonist to express his heroic stature through actions and deeds; in other words, the villain creates conflict, something which the ancient Greek tragedians understood as essential to the denouement or the ultimate solution to the problems within the story itself.

But what exactly is an archetype? Basically, it is not so much a character but a psychic entity, a member of the collective unconscious that is shared by every human being on the planet regardless of race, cultural origin, religious background, or geography. In some ways, an archetype is much like a shadow cast upon the floor; it is also similar to an inherited memory passed down through the generations. These archetypes are also primordial and date back to the beginnings of civilization when humans did not understand the workings of the natural world. So, in order to explain it, a mythological universe was created, filled with supernatural beings that control every aspect of life and death. In addition, archetypes make up the foundation of dreams, both good and bad, and often behave "like ghosts, and then fade away, like spirits on the wind."[2]

Almost all archetypes possess positive and negative traits, much like Leone's "Man With No Name" anti-hero, and can include compassion, love, honor, hate, envy, greed, and vengeance. Two of the most powerful traits are good and evil which have served as the basis for great storytelling down through the ages. This is the battle of the self, powered by the ego, and is symbolized by the hero and the villain. Think of Jekyll and Hyde, Sherlock Holmes and Dr. Moriarty, Dr. Van Helsing and Count Dracula, Dr. Faustus and the devil in the shape of Mephistopheles, and of course, Frank Talby and Scott Mary in *Day of Anger*.

Because archetypes are so ingrained in the human subconscious mind, the traits linked to them invariably end up as literary/film characters, such as Colonel Mortimer as the great teacher, mentor, and "wise old man;" Max Sand (Steve McQueen) in *Nevada Smith* (1966) as the innocent and inexperienced youth; Tuco in *The Good, The Bad, and The Ugly* as the scapegoat and underdog; and Ramon Rojo (Gian Maria Volonte) as the murderous villain in *A Fistful of Dollars*.

When it comes to the three Van Cleef characters discussed in the chapters that follow, the most influential archetype outside of the villain is the mentor, "a positive figure" (more or less) "who aids and/or trains the hero" and is always greatly "enthused" about his role concerning the hero. In effect, to be in the presence of a mentor is to be in the presence of a god, the "higher Self," the "wiser, nobler, more god-like part" of a human being.[3] This mentor as a literary/film character also serves a number of dramatic functions which overall creates and maintains tension and conflict while also reinforcing the motives of the hero/anti-hero or in some instances, the mentor's own motivations.

Some of these functions includes teaching and training (Scott Mary as the hero, Frank Talby as his "bad" teacher with ulterior motives); the giving of a special gift which aids the hero in some way (the Colt revolver with an eight-inch barrel, Talby's "gift" to

Scott Mary, and Mortimer's "gift" of the entire bounty to Manco in *For a Few Dollars More*); motivation directed toward either the hero or the mentor himself (Angel Eyes and his on-going struggles against Blondie in *The Good, The Bad, and The Ugly* in search of the buried gold); and the planting of information or some type of prop of great importance to the outcome of the story (Doc Holliday's Colt revolver, bequeathed to Scott Mary by Murph Allan in *Day of Anger*).[4]

In addition, there are several types of mentors usually found in spaghetti westerns. These would include the dark mentor (Frank Talby and Angel Eyes as the mentor of his gang of bounty killers) who frequently overturns "every conventional heroic value" and "guides the hero on the road to crime and destruction;" the fallen mentor (Colonel Mortimer and Talby) who may be "dealing with the problems of aging" and experiencing "all of the stages of a hero's journey on his own path to redemption;" and most essential, the inner mentor (all of Van Cleef's characters from the three films), "an experienced, hardened character who has no need for a mentor" and represents "the unspoken code of the gunfighter" with internalized notions of honor, both good and bad. Some heroes/anti-heroes might also recall "bits of wisdom" provided by the mentor (Frank Talby's lessons to Scott Mary) which becomes key to solving the problems lurking within the story.[5]

There are also archetypal settings, objects, and landscapes like an open desert devoid of life, certain types of trees, mountains, rivers, the ocean, and even the weather, and specific actions and/or events, a few being conflicts between characters via rejection and bonding; the journey or the quest for wealth and self-identity; the transition or test (the rite of passage); birth/death and rebirth through pain and suffering; and the fall or expulsion from human society.

With few exceptions, a mixture of these archetypes and scenarios are found in every single American/Eurowestern and are instantly recognized via the collective unconscious as mental images when viewing, thinking, or reading about them. But most importantly, they create emotional responses like fear, excitement, surprise, and disgust, which turns film characters into living, breathing, flesh and blood human beings. In effect, the villain as a mythic archetype is dark, shadowy, and mysterious, and symbolizes chaos, cruelty, and disobedience. As Carl Jung, the great Swiss psychiatrist, once remarked, the true villain "tends to openly disobey the rules of society and as expected is more often than not disturbingly fascinating."[6]

It is self-evident that the characters portrayed by Lee Van Cleef are "disturbingly fascinating." One reason is because his on-screen personas appeal to the primitive "id," a term coined by Sigmund Freud more than a hundred years ago during his studies on the human mind. This part of the human subconscious "is of a negative character and can be described only as a contrast to the ego" which allows us to use common sense and reason. Freud refers to the "id" as a place of chaos, "a cauldron full of seething excitations" lacking organization and a collective will and driven by "a striving to bring about satisfaction" in the pursuit of pleasure.[7] This "id" is one of the foundations of true villainy as an insensitive, brutal, and ruthless monster and sadist who gains pleasure from inflicting pain and suffering on others, both physically and emotionally.

In essence, the Eurowestern characters portrayed by Lee Van Cleef in *For a Few Dollars More, The Good, The Bad, and The Ugly*, and *Day of Anger* are mythological characters based on the ancient archetypes of the mentor and the villain, especially Angel Eyes, the consummate spaghetti western sadist who takes great pleasure in slapping defenseless women, inflicting torture on "enemy combatants" in a Union prisoner of war camp, and triumphantly walking out the door after killing Baker (Livio Lorenzon) and his young, rifle-wielding son for $500, a nice "tidy sum" for a hired assassin.

Thus, as a sub-genre, Eurowesterns and Leone's anti-heroic "Man With No Name" trilogy are what Richard Locke calls "hard-boiled westerns" minus all of the sentimentality in favor of criminality, extreme violence, and machismo. These films are also "Hobbesian in nature"[8] or an exultation of life without any form of control or moral foundation, an existential world of nihilistic chaos in which the villain, and sometimes the mentor, makes the life of the hero/anti-hero "solitary, poor, nasty, brutish, and short."[9]

ENDNOTES

1. "How the Western Was Won." *New York Times Magazine.* 2007, 54.
2. Voytilla, Stuart and Christopher Vogler. *Myth and the Movies: Discovering the Mythic Structure.* Studio City, CA: Michael Wiese Books, 1999, 4.
3. Ibid, 47.
4. Voytilla & Vogler, *Myth and the Movies*, 48-51.
5. Ibid, 52-55.
6. Jung, Carl. "Archetypes and the Collective Unconscious." *The Collected Works of C.G. Jung.* Vol. 9. NY: Princeton UP, 1977, 153.
7. *New Introductory Lectures on Psychoanalysis.* NY: W.W. Norton, 1995, 174.
8. "Grand Horse Opera: The Best Westerns Celebrate Our History and Criticize the Ugly Stereotypes of the Genre." *American Scholar*, 77.3 (1998): 135.
9. Shaplin, Adriano. *The Tragedy of Thomas Hobbes.* NY: Oberon Books, 2009, 175.

The Gunfighter and the Bounty Hunter: Fact Vs. Fiction

From a cinematic viewpoint, every spaghetti western, and especially Sergio Leone's "Man With No Name" trilogy, is saturated with imagery of the Old West during a time when the United States was expanding beyond the Mississippi River and into the vastness of the American Southwest. This period is generally fixed between the beginning of the American Civil War in 1861, the bloodiest and most violent conflict of the nineteenth century, and 1877, when the great American railroad system stretched to the shores of the Pacific Ocean, making it possible to travel from the Eastern Seaboard and the Deep South to Arizona and California in less than a week. But by 1879, following the great economic panic some five years earlier, most Americans who had "unquestionably accepted the results of the Civil War as insurance" for a prolonged episode of economic boom, "were severely shaken, and never regained their full confidence" in what we now refer to as the American Dream.[1]

Also, in the eyes of many Americans, the frontiers of the Far West offered "great open expanses for personal development and opportunity,"[2] particularly for white settlers from the Midwest, seeking land for farming and homesteading, and Eastern entrepreneurs in search of new sources of income, such as cattle and mining, and ways to exploit the burgeoning populations in towns being built alongside the railroads. But in the early 1880s, coincidentally at about the same time as the famous gunfight at the OK Corral between Virgil, Morgan, and Wyatt Earp, Doc Holliday, and the Clanton gang in Tombstone, Arizona, it was becoming obvious that the American frontier was rapidly disappearing. According to Goldwin Smith, a prominent British-Canadian historian and journalist writing in 1877,

"The youth of the American Republic is over; and maturity, with its burdens, difficulties, and anxieties, has surely arrived."[3]

Along with the settlers, most of whom were of European ancestry, and those desiring to take advantage of the American frontier shortly after the close of the Civil War during a period known as Reconstruction (1866 to 1877), another figure crept onto the scene with different motivations and as compared to "normal" social conformists possessed certain mental deviations which "excluded him from the mainstream of society."[4] This figure was the gunfighter, the gunslinger, the man with the holstered Colt "Peacemaker," the "solitary, self-sufficient" stranger with a "shadowy background," the kind of man who knew exactly what he wanted and how to go about getting it, whether inside or outside of the law.

Cinematically, this figure is known as the "heavy," the "bad guy," a character with "a gruff voice, stubbled face, and a hair-trigger temper,"[5] sporting an attitude of utter contempt for not only society but almost everyone living within it, including those who represent law and order in the form of the town marshal or sheriff. In this context, the lines become somewhat blurred regarding the personality of the screen villain and that of the actor. But with Lee Van Cleef, it is quite simple—he *is* the villain, a special kind of actor with the ability to transcend the character on the scripted page and inject his own personality into it. In so many words, this type of actor does not act; he is, in fact, the character itself in the physical form of the actor. This is why Lee Van Cleef is the "Best of the Bad."

Over the last one hundred years or so, a vast amount of material has been written about historical gunfighters and their supposedly "quick draw" abilities to shoot a man dead in the blink of an eye, a few being *The Red-Blooded Heroes of the Frontier* by Edgar B. Bronson (1910); *Arizona's Dark and Bloody Ground* by Earle Forrest (1953); *The Bad Man of the West* by George Hendricks (1950); and *Wild Bill Hickok: The Prince of Pistoleers* by Frank Wilstach (1926), plus an entire slew of magazine articles, contemporary newspaper accounts, and biographies written by shady journalists from the East, the so-called "dime novels" that contained more fiction (if not pure fabrication) than fact. One of the most popular of these journalists was E.C.Z. Judson, also known as Ned Buntline, who allegedly "invented" the long-barreled revolver used with such great precision by Colonel Mortimer in *For a Few Dollars More*.

Traditionally, the period between the end of the Civil War in 1865 and the infamous shoot-out at the OK Corral in 1881 represents the era of the gunfighter, most of whom were born sometime around 1835 when settlers traveling to the Pacific Coast and the Northwest were following the Oregon Trail. Coincidentally, it was in 1835 that Samuel Colt patented the breech-loading, folding trigger revolver called the Paterson pistol, the forerunner of American-made percussion pistols used during the Civil War and later on the famous Colt "Peacemaker," the pistol that forever changed the American West and how men settled their disputes over land, money, and sometimes women.

Despite what Hollywood has depicted in motion pictures concerning the gunfighter over the last eighty odd years, more than a third died of natural causes and a large number managed to survive well into their sixties and seventies. Of the number that did end up dying a violent death, the average age was around thirty-five. Not surprisingly, most professional gunfighters perished in states and territories with the highest amount of shootings with Texas leading the way, followed by Kansas, New Mexico, Oklahoma, California, Missouri, and Colorado.[6] Although statistical figures are unreliable, it has been estimated that between 1870 and 1889, a mere three hundred actual gunfights occurred in the "Wild West" involving outlaws, hired guns, and/or bounty hunters.[7] This number by itself is not at all staggering, considering that tens of thousands of men packed a six-shooter on a daily basis and lived in very unstable places like El Paso, Kansas City, Dodge City, Sacramento, and Denver. As proof of this instability, a reporter for the *New York Tribune* stated in 1882 that in the town of Abilene, Texas, "There is no law, no restraint, in this seething cauldron of vice and depravity."[8]

In effect, the gunfighter's legendary proficiency with a six-shooter is highly over-rated, yet it is still believed, due in part to the popularity of the Hollywood western and its counterpart the Eurowestern, that gunfighters were "gifted with phenomenal reflexes which enabled them to draw and fire a revolver with incredible speed and accuracy."[9] This conjures up images of the "Man With No Name" and Frank Talby with his specially-modified Colt for "thumbing" the hammer with rapid dexterity. Another result of Hollywood's intentional aberration of the gunfighter is that he "held the power of life and death in his hands and used guns" to solve a myriad of problems,[10] such as eliminating rivals or the town marshal with an arrest warrant in his pocket. In reality, the gunfighter was no different than anyone else, except for perhaps having a reputation as a cold-blooded killer with black cat luck on his side when it came to facing down an adversary in the street or the local saloon.

In some historical accounts of supposedly real gunfighters, they always "avoided dark alleyways and the direct glare of street lamps," and indoors always stood or sat with their backs against the wall, and because of living on "the edge of self-destruction for so long, their faces wore a fixed expression of pain and misery,"[11] making it rather simple to spot them in a crowded barroom. Of course, all of this is pure exaggeration and suggests that early movie gunfighters were the precursors to characters usually found in the genre of film noir of the 1940s and 1950s, such as a man in a raincoat walking silently down a darkened street with a hat pulled over his eyes and glancing furtively at a stranger standing in the shadowed doorway of a sleazy bar or a run-down apartment building.

Shortly after the end of the Civil War, referred to in the Deep South as "The War Between the States," thousands of ex-soldiers, both Union and Confederate, gathered up what few belonging they still possessed and headed out west, usually by horseback or as a member of a wagon train. Some of these men were well-trained in the use of firearms as a result of fighting in numerous bloody battles and had become "immune to feelings of guilt about killing a man"[12] when it was required in order to survive. However, some of these ex-soldiers, their homes and families destroyed during the war, turned to the life of an outlaw, haunted by terrible memories of the past and filled with greed and arrogance, thus making him "a taker rather than a giver." Certainly, due to an immersion in violence and death, this type of "bad man" was openly "selfish, and willing to kill to get what he wanted" and firmly believed that his own needs and wants came first.[13]

Joseph G. Rosa, considered as an authority on the life and times of James Butler "Wild Bill" Hickok and a meticulous researcher dedicated to facts instead of fabrication, provides an excellent summation on the true gunfighter, the proverbial "bad man" as depicted in hundreds of Hollywood films and those "dime novels" of the late 1880s and 1890s:

Thousands of men drifted westward after the Civil War, dreaming of riches that remained elusive. Disillusioned, they went to great lengths to achieve wealth with a minimum of effort, (and) gambled, fought, and robbed to get what they wanted. Some killed, (and) each subsequent killing became easier. Eventually, many died in violence among people who cared little for them or for their sudden end.[14]

As to the bounty hunter, this sub-branch of the historical gunfighter is far more elusive because of the absence of reliable documentation and the fact that the actual names of these "man-killers" and their places of origin were never recorded. Basically, the Old West bounty hunter as portrayed in countless Hollywood and spaghetti westerns is a myth; however, as the old premise goes, all myths are based on varying degrees of fact, depending on the original source and the time frame in which they are set. At the mythological core is American cinema and its long output of westerns, beginning in 1903 with *The Great Train Robbery*, a ten-minute long, one-reeler directed and photographed by Edwin S. Porter, a former cameraman for Thomas Edison. The first American western to fully incorporate the "man-killer" motif was *The Bounty Hunter* (1954), directed by Andre de Toth with Randolph Scott whom Van Cleef had worked with in *Ride Lonesome* in 1958. The one-sheet movie poster for this film says it all—"When the law puts up the money, the Bounty Hunter puts on his guns!"[15]

Pinning down the first spaghetti western takes a bit more digging and of course depends on who you ask. According to the Spaghetti Western Database, the earliest Italian/Spanish Eurowestern appears to be *La sceriffa* ("The Sheriff Was a Lady" in the US), a comedic revenge yarn released on August 16, 1959 and directed by Roberto Bianchi Montero. There is also *Il terrore dell'Oklahoma* ("The Terror of Oklahoma" in the US), concerning a gang of outlaws terrorizing a small western town, released two months later in October and directed by Mario Amendola. Interestingly, this film featured Benito Stefanelli, a Eurowestern veteran who also appeared in *The Good, The Bad, and The Ugly, Day of Anger*, and *For a Few Dollars More*.

And then there is *Tierra Brutal* ("The Savage Guns" in the US), a Spanish production released in October of 1962 and directed by Michael Carreras of Hammer Films, along with Hammer screenwriter Jimmy Sangster as co-producer. Shot in Almeria, Spain and with locations in the famous Tabernas Desert, *Savage Guns*, starring Richard Basehart as gunslinger Steve Fallon, fits well into the historical arena of the gunfighter, due to being set after the Civil War and having a former Confederate officer (Don Taylor) as its main protagonist.

This film is a prototype to what came later via Sergio Leone and his "Man With No Name" films with their white-washed adobe houses, grizzled and beady-eyed bandits, desert locations, and most appropriately, "the iconic, mysterious gunslinger who finds himself between two warring factions." [16] As a side note, *Savage Guns* also features a number of secondary Italian character actors who went on to appear in many spaghetti westerns. However, since *La sceriffa, Il terrore dell'Oklahoma,* and *Savage Guns* do not feature full-blown bounty hunter characters, *A Fistful of Dollars* still remains as the first "man-killer" extravaganza with Eastwood as the anti-hero which in the opinion of Joseph G. Rosa "certainly damages the legendary image of the gunfighter" with its "character of unrelenting evil" that is truly removed from reality. [17]

As previously mentioned, reliable documentation concerning true-to-life bounty hunters of the Old West is practically non-existent; however, several extensive biographies have been written over the last forty years on real-life bounty hunter Charlie Siringo, born in 1855 in Matagorda County, Texas, of Italian/Irish parentage. As Benjamin E. Pingenot relates, Siringo worked as a cowboy in the coastal plains region of Texas between 1871 and 1872 for several big cattle barons and became a trail driver on the Chisholm Trail in 1876. A few years later, Siringo helped to establish the LX Ranch in Dodge City and as a hired ranch hand met Billy the Kid (a.k.a. Henry McCarty). At some point, Siringo led a posse into New Mexico in pursuit of Billy the Kid and his gang. In 1884, he left the life of a cowboy and became a merchant in Caldwell, Kansas, where he began to write his memoirs about his days in the Old West. In 1886, Siringo relocated to Chicago and joined the famous Pinkerton's National Detective Agency. [18]

As an employee of the Pinkerton Agency, Siringo became a bona fide bounty hunter and spent twenty-two years tracking hundreds of men wanted dead or alive into the wilds of northern Alaska and deep into the rugged terrain of southern Mexico. As a gun-toting bounty hunter, Siringo was "reputed to be a fine shot, (and) was proud of the fact that he made most of his arrests without violence."[19] In 1907, Siringo retired from Pinkerton's Agency and decided to start writing books about his bounty hunting adventures and some of the outlaws he had encountered over the years. After the publication of a scathing indictment against the Pinkerton Agency in 1915, Siringo was appointed by the governor of New Mexico as a ranger and served two years in active service against cattle rustlers.[20]

In 1922, with failing health and living in dire poverty, Siringo moved to Los Angeles, hoping to make some type of income from the sales of his books. Several years later, he became friends with silent film star William S. Hart, the original western cowboy actor, and appeared in numerous bit roles. In 1927, he published his last memoir *Riata and Spurs* which the Pinkerton Agency objected to because of Siringo's detailed coverage of secretive agency procedures. After his death in 1928, Siringo became somewhat of a legend and is now seen as "the quintessential cowboy and determined bounty hunter" who greatly assisted in the romanticization of the Old West and the creation of various myths linked to it.[21]

Although Charlie Siringo was indeed a true bounty hunter or a "cowboy detective" as he preferred to call himself, and possessed nerves of steel and a crafty mind, he did not exhibit in any way the prime personality trait of all cinematic bounty hunters—the cold-blooded willingness to kill anyone who stands in the way of obtaining money, power, influence, or revenge. Also, Siringo was not driven by the characteristics so often attached to cinematic bounty hunters, namely, "arrogance, an indifference to human life, and the destructive emotions of anger, resentment, and jealousy."[22] Lastly, despite carrying and deftly using a six-shooter, invariably a Colt "Peacemaker" slung low on his right hip, Siringo was not a gunfighter as contrasted with such notorious figures as Billy the Kid, James Riley, Ben Thompson (who allegedly killed more than forty men during his lifetime), and James Butler "Wild Bill" Hickok.

Unfortunately, the absence of reliable documentation makes it next to impossible to write a narrative on true-to-life bounty hunters of the Old West based on fact rather than cinematic fantasy. In essence, historical accounts on bounty hunters like Charlie Siringo and a small handful of others who actually lived the life of a "man-killer" brings up the possibility that men similar to Colonel Mortimer and Frank Talby might have actually lived and were involved in events comparable to those depicted in *For a Few Dollars More* and *Day of Anger*; however, proof of the existence of these types of men roaming the American Southwest in search of bounty is currently not available, nor is it likely that such proof will come to the surface any time soon.

ENDNOTES

1. La Feber, Walter. *The New Empire: An Interpretation of American Expansion*, 1860-1898. Ithaca, NY: Cornell University Press, 1998, 14.
2. Ibid, 11.
3. Ibid, 16.
4. Horner, William R. *Bad at the Bijou*. Jefferson, NC: McFarland & Company, 1982, 11.
5. Ibid, 12.
6. Chinn, Stephen, Kenneth Thomas, and the Kansas Heritage Group. Kansas Gunfighters. Internet, 2010.
7. Ibid, Internet.
8. Nolan, Frederick. *Wild West: History, Myth, and the Making of America*. Secaucus, NJ: Chartwell Books, 2004, 186.
9. Rosa, Joseph G. *The Gunfighter: Man or Myth?* Oklahoma City: University of Oklahoma Press, 1969, 5.
10. Ibid, 11.
11. Ibid, 12.
12. Ibid, 40.
13. Ibid, 42.
14. Ibid, 42.
15. Leonard, Elmore, and Louis L'Amour. *Western Movies: Classic Wild West Films*. UK: Severn House, Ltd., 1997, 23.
16. Internet Movie Database, 2010.
17. *The Gunfighter: Man or Myth?* 211.
18. Charles Angelo Siringo. *The Handbook of Texas Online*. Internet, 2010.
19. Ibid, Internet.
20. Ibid, Internet.
21. Nolan, *Wild West*, 223.
22. Rosa, *The Gunfighter*, 164.

The Guns of Lee Van Cleef

"A gun is a tool, no better or no worse than any other tool, an axe, a shovel. A gun is only as good or as bad as the man using it."
Alan Ladd as Shane (1953)

Since the days of the Revolutionary War when American colonists took up arms against the tyranny and oppression of the British Empire and the monarchy of King George III, there has existed what some refer to as a "gun cult" in the United States, a type of worship over a simple piece of hardware or as Shane describes it, a kind of tool that is no different than an axe, a shovel, or a hammer, all designed to serve a particular purpose, such as chopping wood, digging a ditch, or pounding a nail into a wall. However, unlike these kinds of tools which could be used as weapons, a gun only serves one specific function—to kill a living thing, whether a bear, a deer, or a human being. Of course, a gun can also serve as a form of protection or as a deterrent to a threat made upon someone by another person. From a logical viewpoint, a gun lying on a table or hanging over a fireplace does not pose any kind of a threat unless someone picks it up, cocks it, aims, and fires, thus either wounding or killing the unfortunate person in the line of the bullet's trajectory. Therefore, as Shane so accurately puts it, "A gun is only as good or as bad as the man using it," a simple and straightforward observation without much room for argument.

In early 1978, Lee Van Cleef, while sitting at his dining room table at his home in the San Fernando Valley, was asked by an interviewer how he felt about guns. "GUNS! I have some guns here at home and I keep them loaded to protect myself,"[1] he says which is an indictment against strangers who over the years have attempted to test Van Cleef's "tough guy" image by picking fights with him in Los Angeles bars while minding his own business and enjoying a glass of whiskey. He adds that when he was ten years old, his father introduced him to guns, most probably for hunting in the wilds of New Jersey. Apparently, Van Cleef was also quite good with the old-fashioned "quick draw," for he recounts that during the filming of an unidentified western, "I was doing a scene, and the director said, " I can't see the draw." This was because I'd drawn, cocked, and fired in 1/8 of a second."[2] There is also the long-circulating anecdote concerning a friendly argument between Van Cleef and Clint Eastwood on the set of *The Good, The Bad, and The Ugly* about which one is the fastest draw. Although undocumented, it seems that Van Cleef won out after being clocked frame by frame.

In his spaghetti western film roles, Lee Van Cleef utilizes a wide variety of guns, ranging from Winchester rifles to several different types and models of revolvers and pistols, most notably the Colt .45 "Peacemaker" in *Day of Anger* and *For a Few Dollars More*, and the Remington 1858 New Army .44 caliber and Colt 1851 Navy as seen in *The Good, The Bad, and The Ugly*. In regards to the Civil War period and the Old West, these three firearms are historically important, for they were much more than mere hardware or tools for the men who depended on them for survival in a harsh world. In fact, these and similar revolvers were so pivotal in the everyday lives of the gunfighter and the bounty hunter that they became physical extensions, i.e., a gunfighter without his pistol would sooner than later end up in the cemetery. Then there is the question of skill in the use of a "six-shooter." As Bat Masterson once quipped, skill or the ability to use a pistol is invariably inborn, but "There were plenty of men who learned to shoot simply because they had to. Every gunman who was not a reasonably good shot went back to where he came from and quickly."[3]

In the hands of a competent and skilled gunslinger like Colonel Mortimer and Frank Talby, the gun symbolizes his masculinity and rugged individualism and serves as an implement for bestowing self-imposed justice and destruction. Without a doubt, the Colt .45 "Peacemaker" was the weapon of choice for many gunfighters and due to its popularity was dubbed "Judge Colt and his jury of six,"[4] a six-shot, single action, 250 grain cartridge revolver that had to be cocked each time for firing. With a fully loaded weight of just over three pounds, the Colt .45 was hard-hitting and deadly. At ten yards, a .45 caliber lead slug, after entering a person's body, would leave behind a relatively small hole which was often hard to find because of overlapping layers of clothing, but upon turning the person over, the exit wound, due to the mushrooming of the lead slug, was immediately noticeable at about the size of a half dollar. More than likely, any opponent shot above the waist would not have survived because of a great loss of blood and severe internal injuries.

Historically, in 1868, a gun designer for the Samuel Colt Company patented a new type of loading system as compared to the old-fashioned muzzle-loading revolvers of the Civil War era, also known as percussion cap and ball. This new system allowed cartridges to be front-loaded into the cylinder and ejected by an attachment linked to the hammer. However, this system failed to live up to its expectations and was quickly discontinued by the Colt Company. At about the same time, Colt designers figured out a way to convert old cap and ball revolvers to accept rim and center fire cartridges by replacing the traditional cap and ball cylinder with one that could be loaded via a swinging side gate attached to the frame of the pistol with an ejector rod for manually removing spent cartridges. In 1873, this type of loading system led to the creation of the New Model Army .45 caliber revolver, the proverbial "Peacemaker."

Produced by the Colt Company with calibers ranging from .45 to .476, the "Peacemaker" became the most popular pistol ever made, and in 1878, due to public demand, Colt introduced the Frontier model which was chambered to accept .44-40 caliber cartridges used in the 1873 model Winchester side-loading rifle. Barrel lengths varied from five and a half to seven and a half inches, and some gunfighters sawed off two inches of barrel length from the seven and half model and were known to file off the front sights and the very top edge of the hammer, normally made with grooves which prevented the thumb from slipping when cocking it. Exactly why some gunfighters decided to cut off two inches of barrel from the seven and a half model is not clear, but it could be related to the balance of the longer-barreled version. American gunsmith David R. Chicoine suggests that due to the muzzle end of the barrel becoming flared because of some kind of obstruction, the damaged area would be cut off to make the gun usable.

These home-made adjustments created a type of pseudo-myth related to what is called "fanning" where the hammer was either thumbed (Frank Talby in *Day of Anger*) or fanned with the edge of the hand, almost always the right. How this "fanning" method worked is quite simple. The first shot was accomplished by pulling the trigger which was then held down while the hand fanned the hammer, allowing the cylinder to spin freely. However, this firing method was inaccurate and was useful only at close range, perhaps less than ten yards. Basically, this method is a spaghetti western fabrication and is solidly ingrained through images of Clint Eastwood "fanning" his Colt .45 and killing four or five men "as quick as light." However, there are "quick-draw" artists of today who specialize in "fanning" and compete in shooting contests for big cash prizes and much notoriety.

In *For a Few Dollars More*, Colonel Mortimer possesses an entire collection of guns, kept close at hand in a rolled-up leather bundle on his horse. In one scene, he unfolds this bundle to reveal a strange-looking weapon with a barrel that appears to be two feet long. This was known as the Buntline Special or the Colt .45 caliber, single-action Army revolver which supposedly was used by Wyatt Earp as marshal of Tombstone, Arizona. According to legend, this firearm was originally commissioned in 1876 by Ned Buntline (a pseudonym for Edward Judson), best-known for "inventing" the pulp dime novel and writing highly-exaggerated accounts on famous gunfighters of the Old West like Earp, Hickok, and Masterson. This particular pistol, the "Colt Buntline," was available in three barrel lengths—ten, twelve, and sixteen inches, along with a detachable, metal skeleton stock that could be affixed to the grip with thumb screws. In *For a Few Dollars More*, Colonel Mortimer uses this same weapon on a number of occasions but instead with a Winchester-style wooden stock. Whether this type of stock was actually available from Colt has not been determined.

However, unlike the typical Colt .45 "Peacemaker," the so-called Buntline Special could only be purchased by special order from the Colt factory in Hartford, Connecticut. Records from 1878 reveal that a certain C.G. Wingard ordered two of these Buntline Specials with ten inch barrels that were re-chambered at the factory to accept .44 caliber shells. As to Mr. Buntline, there is no evidence to support the idea that he ever owned a "Colt Buntline," nor that he had anything to do with its design. As William B. Shillingberg relates, the eccentric Mr. Buntline never supplied Wyatt Earp or any other gunfighter with this type of firearm, nor did he have any connections with these revolvers which is why the Colt Company "never referred to them as Buntline Specials."[5]

Since the story line of *The Good, The Bad, and The Ugly* is set during the Civil War, circa 1864, one of the guns of choice for Angel Eyes is the Remington New Army 1858 .44 caliber revolver which along with the Colt .36 caliber single or double-action Navy "Dragoon" was extremely popular with Union and Confederate soldiers and served admirably in a number of important battles, such as Cold Harbor in Virginia, where over 7,000 men were killed in less than twenty minutes.[6] Originally designed as a percussion cap and ball pistol, the Remington New Army 1858, along with its counterpart the 1863 New Model, underwent many alterations over the years, and as gun design advanced, it too was modified to accept cartridges via a swinging side gate built into the frame.

This alteration did not become widely available until 1875 with the Remington .44-40 caliber model; however, near the end of the Civil War, high-ranking Union officers proudly wore this modified version, making it a rare exception to the standard cap and ball pistol. In fact, because of its superior design and dependability, many Union as well as Confederate officers purchased this revolver with their own money. As an added benefit, brand-new Remington Army models often came with an extra cylinder which could be kept pre-loaded in a pocket. Between 1862 and 1865, the peak years of the Civil War, more than 115,000 Remington 1863 cap and ball revolvers were produced at a price of about $15 and were sold throughout the country, especially west of the Mississippi River which at the time was being flooded with settlers from the East and former soldiers seeking fame and fortune. However, modified 1858 and 1863 Remington models were just beginning to appear as a result of advances in design made by gunsmiths working for Remington Arms in Ilion, New York.[7]

Angel Eyes also carries a Colt 1851 .36 caliber Navy revolver that has been modified to accept cartridges as contrasted with his muzzle-loading 1858 Remington New Army. Along with the familiar Colt .44 caliber "Dragoon" Army cap and ball revolver which was quite ponderous, the Colt Navy was lighter, better balanced, and aesthetically pleasing. During the Civil War, the Colt Company supplied the Union with more than 17,000 Navy revolvers, thus making it a Union-issued firearm for troops and officers in the field. As might be suspected, "a captured Yankee Colt Navy was much prized by Confederate soldiers"[8] who were often equipped with substandard firearms, due to the inability of the Confederate army to purchase weapons from Union gun manufacturers and a shortage of gun-making factories and materials. This particular single-action revolver weighed two and a half pounds and came from the Colt factory with a 7 1/2 inch octagon barrel, and although chambered at .36 caliber, it was hard-hitting and deadly accurate.

As a director, Sergio Leone possessed a deep passion for historical accuracy and did everything possible in line with his budget to convey the closest approximation to reality or at least as he perceived it through the lenses of his camera and his own imagination. Leone also did a great deal of research before the cameras began to roll and was known to have been a perfectionist. In 1960, prior to making the first "Man With No Name" film, Leone consulted Aldo Uberti, a well-known gun maker in Italy and a specialist in Old West firearms, to make certain that the guns utilized in his films would be as accurate as possible. This consultation with Uberti paid off handsomely, for the guns used by Lee Van Cleef in *For a Few Dollars More* and *The Good, The Bad, and The Ugly* are excellent representations of real firearms. Not surprisingly, Uberti's replicas of the Colt .45 "Peacemaker," and the Colt 1851 Navy and Remington 1858 New Army revolvers were so amazingly real that almost every spaghetti western filmmaker followed suit and used Uberti's gun replicas for their own films, including Tonino Valerii in *Day of Anger* and Luciano Vincenzoni in *Death Rides a Horse*.

The three characters portrayed by Lee Van Cleef in *For a Few Dollars More, The Good, The Bad, and The Ugly,* and *Day of Anger* represent the finest spaghetti western gunslingers to ever appear in the cinema, and because of Van Cleef's superb acting ability to bring a character to life, one is almost led to believe that they are real, rather than fictional shadows of true-to-life gunfighters. When augmented with the use of guns, Colonel Mortimer, Angel Eyes, and Frank Talby become living, breathing human beings with fully-developed personalities, and much like the gunfighters and bounty hunters of the historical American West, these three men followed some simple rules founded on instinct and experience and carried a gun for two main reasons—first, to survive and second, to help them accomplish their individual goals, fueled by vengeance, greed, and a lust for power.

ENDNOTES

1. Wilson, Earl. "Van Cleef Works at Keeping His 'Mean SOB' Reputation." *Sarasota Herald Tribune*. January 31, 1978, p. 12-A.
2. Ibid, p. 12-A.
3. Rosa, *The Gunfighter*, 179.
4. Ibid, 5.
5. "Wyatt Earp and the 'Buntline Special' Myth." *Kansas Historical Quarterly*. Vol. 42 no. 2, 1976: 113-154.
6. McPherson, *Battle Cry of Freedom*, 245.
7. Edwards, William B. *Civil War Guns*. Secaucus, NJ: Castle Books, 1982, 231.
8. Rosa, 39.

Photo Gallery

Van Cleef as Angel Eyes, *The Good, The Bad, and The Ugly*

Van Cleef as Colonel Mortimer, *For a Few Dollars More*

Van Cleef as Colonel Mortimer, *For a Few Dollars More*

Van Cleef as Frank Talby, *Day of Anger*

Van Cleef as Angel Eyes, *The Good, The Bad, and The Ugly*

Van Cleef's gravesite, Forest Lawn Cemetery, Los Angeles

Van Cleef and Giuliano Gemma, *Day of Anger*

Real-life bounty hunter Charlie Siringo, circa 1890

Wild West City, NJ, with Van Cleef atop the stagecoach.
COURTESY OF THE SOMERVILLE PUBLIC LIBRARY

Van Cleef, 1960. With all of his fingers intact!
COURTESY OF CHRISTOPHER GULLO.

THE GUNMEN
COLONEL DOUGLAS MORTIMER: VENGEANCE IS MINE!

On April 10, 1865, General Robert E. Lee issued General Order No. 9 in the form of a letter to the Army of Northern Virginia in which he commends his troops for their "unsurpassed courage and fortitude" on the battlefield. Lee also tells his men that they are free to return to their homes, knowing they have performed their duties faithfully against a mighty enemy. In closing, Lee thanks his men for sticking by his side and then "with grateful remembrance of your kind and generous consideration," he bids them a fond farewell with the hope that their lives can somehow be repaired and that their loved ones will welcome them home with open arms and great affection.[1]

This letter officially ended the Civil War following Lee's surrender to General Ulysses S. Grant, the commander of all Union forces, at Appomattox Courthouse on April 9, 1865. As the worst national catastrophe in the history of the United States, the "War Between the States" resulted in the complete destruction of the Old South and its antebellum system of slavery. More men were killed in this four year-long conflict than all other American wars combined with estimated Union and Confederate losses at more than 500,000, most being under the age of thirty. Soldiers from the Deep South who managed to survive without serious injury found their homes and families gone, their lands destroyed, and all of their possessions either stolen, burned, or confiscated by Union troops. In essence, the lives they knew before the war had vanished, were literally "Gone With the Wind" as Margaret Mitchell wrote in her monumental 1936 novel, leaving behind nothing but bitter memories and for some a longing for vengeance.

One of the hardest hit states in the Confederacy was South Carolina, where the capital city of Columbia was burned to the ground during General Sherman's famous March to the Sea in February of 1865. It has been rumored that Union soldiers, after supplying themselves with stolen liquor, began to drink heavily and set a number of fires which were fanned by high winds across the city. On February 18, Sherman ordered that all buildings, railroad depots, warehouses, factories, and private businesses with any military value be destroyed; a number of mansions within the city and in the surrounding countryside were also looted, then burned down, including the old South Carolina State House, built in 1790.[2]

It is from this type of environment that Douglas Mortimer emerged as a colonel in the Confederate army, a high-ranking officer in command of a state regiment of volunteers from South Carolina. As a true "Southern gentleman," Mortimer possesses many outstanding qualities, such as loyalty, a guiding sense of duty, and a set of morals indelibly linked to what is known as Southern honor, based on long-standing traditions on how a man should act, think, and behave in Southern society. Part of this Southern honor is deeply rooted in traditional family structure and kinship, being the extended family of brothers and sisters and the bloodline of grandparents and great grandparents.

The male members, especially elder brothers, bear the most honor in regard to making certain that family members are not dishonored through slander, false accusations, or unethical behavior by out-siders. When his sister is raped by El Indio, a vicious bandit and wanted killer, Mortimer takes it upon himself to seek revenge for her death which is made even worse when she kills herself. But El Indio also steals something precious to Mortimer and his family—a gold pocket watch (a matched pair) with chimes, a special gift from his sister's husband who also is killed by El Indio in the couple's bedroom. Therefore, because his family was dishonored through the actions of El Indio, Mortimer departs from his home, circa the early 1870s, in search of revenge with the goal being to kill El Indio, retrieve the gold pocket watch and his family honor.

But in order to survive and perhaps as a way of hastening his search for El Indio, Mortimer becomes a bounty hunter, a "man-killer" equipped with an entire arsenal of weapons and the ability to use them to his own advantage. Mortimer's experience and knowledge concerning guns is quite evident as is his appreciation for what they can accomplish, especially under the worst of conditions when death is represented by a gun barrel hovering only inches away or a bullet ricocheting off a nearby wall.

It all lies within his past as the "best shot in the Carolinas," a talent that could only have been acquired as a sharpshooter in McGowan's Brigade of South Carolinians, a provisional unit created in January of 1863 under the command of Captain William T. Haskell, "a man and officer of the highest caliber and greatly regarded by his comrades in the Confederate Army,"[3] killed in action at the Battle of Gettysburg on July 2, 1863. All of the hand-picked members of this brigade, composed of three companies with forty men each, had proven marksmanship with a weapon, usually the British Pattern 1853 Enfield rifle, a single-shot muzzle-loader bored to .577 caliber and prized for its long range and accuracy in the hands of a competent sniper. This type of firearm was only issued to the top shooters in each company which was determined through shooting competitions.[4] In addition, some of these sharpshooters served as field scouts before the fighting began and would use a collapsible telescope to spy on enemy activities. Mortimer uses this same type of telescope through an open window at his hotel in El Paso, where he first encounters Manco, staying in a cockroach-infested hotel directly across the street.

Although Mortimer is a full-fledged bounty hunter with a penchant for killing and collecting large sums of cash as payment for his "job," he nonetheless is heroic in stature or perhaps anti-heroic, due to his casualness and indifference to killing for money. But his true personality and moral foundation comes to the surface when he decides to give Manco all of the reward money, totaling some $35,000, for El Indio and his gang, plus leaving behind the money stolen from the bank in El Paso. As Richard Locke sees it, Mortimer's only true motivation is to reclaim his murdered sister's honor, symbolized by the gold pocket watch which contains a small miniature photo of his deceased sister. As a result, Manco "calmly stacks twenty-seven bodies in the back of a buckboard and drives off"[5] as Mortimer heads for home to the Carolinas, where his fate remains unknown.

Although acts of vengeance are usually frowned upon by society, due to being driven by selfishness and a giant ego, Colonel Douglas Mortimer conclusively shows that vengeance is sometimes quite acceptable, particularly when the motivation is to restore treasured family honor or to bring closure to a situation initially created by another individual out of sheer perversity. In this respect, vengeance belongs exclusively to Mortimer, for it is his reward for being so dedicated to his Southern principles and to the brave Confederate comrades he left behind on the battlefields of Gettysburg.

ANGEL EYES:
200,000 REASONS TO KILL

All of the outstanding personality traits of Colonel Douglas Mortimer are totally absent when it comes to Angel Eyes or Setenza, a man without any moral foundation, a true villain in every sense of the word who seems to have a talent for making the lives of everyone he encounters "nasty, brutish, and short." In effect, Angel Eyes is the quintessential "bad man," a remorseless killer who thrives on violence and death, a "mean son of a bitch"[6] with a sadistic smile whose primary objective is to obtain $200,000 in stolen Confederate gold, motivated by insatiable greed and the willingness to commit cold-blooded, premeditated murder.

One of his most villainous traits is his indifference to the world around him at a time when the Civil War was raging and thousands of men were dying on the battlefields of Gettysburg, Antietam, Cold Harbor, and Shiloh. This indifference to death and dying is so pronounced that Angel Eyes uses it to his own advantage by having prisoners of war tortured and maimed while under the guise of a Union sergeant in order to discover the location of Jackson (a.k.a. Bill Carson) who hid the stolen Confederate gold in a grave in Sad Hill Cemetery. He is also indifferent to killing and has no qualms about murdering opponents, such as Stevens who pays him $1000 to kill Baker, his rival for the $200,000 in gold, who then proceeds to pay Angel Eyes to kill Stevens. Both men end up dead with Baker shot at point blank through a dirty pillow covering his face as Angel Eyes smiles wickedly and keeps pulling the trigger of his .36 caliber

Navy revolver. After all, "I always follow my job through. You know that."

As a paid gunman, Angel Eyes is also a sadist to the utmost degree and clearly relishes in causing pain and suffering on other human beings. Besides torturing enemy prisoners of war to obtain information about Bill Carson and the hiding place of the Confederate gold, and having Tuco almost beaten to death while handcuffed to a chair, Angel Eyes savagely slaps a young prostitute after fooling her into thinking that Bill Carson is waiting in the darkness of her run-down hotel room. With a trickle of blood oozing down her chin, the prostitute, after relating the whereabouts of Bill Carson, is casually thrown aside, another hapless victim caught up in a web of deceit and treachery devised by Angel Eyes. Interestingly, Van Cleef makes it clear to interviewer William R. Horner that "I don't pound women. I haven't slapped a woman yet on screen." However, Horner counters by mentioning that Angel Eyes does savagely slap and backhand the prostitute in her sleazy hotel room. "That was done by a stuntman," replies Van Cleef, "because I refused to do it."[7]

Although not immediately recognizable, Angel Eyes is the supreme coward, an unheroic trait for a man who externally appears fearless and laughs at death, but internally quivers nervously with apprehension and dread. An excellent example of this cowardice occurs when Angel Eyes hires some of his "friends" as paid assassins to help hunt down Bill Carson, but in the course of events, they all end up being killed by Blondie and Tuco. Angel Eyes, of course, escapes and feels no empathy or pity for his "friends" lying dead in the street. Emanating from deep down inside his black soul, Angel Eyes prefers to let someone else do all of the dirty work while he stands triumphantly in the background, gloating over his success and his talents for deception and manipulation.

One final aspect of his personality is that Angel Eyes prides himself on always finishing an "assignment" with the callousness of a true sociopath. After shooting Stevens through the top of a table holding bowls of food from which he had just finished eating as a "guest," Angel Eyes casually scoops up the $1000, satisfied that he has brought closure to his deal with Stevens, now lying dead on the stone floor. But since Stevens paid Angel Eyes to kill Baker, he feels obligated to return to Baker's filthy, cramped hovel and kill him without mercy or remorse just before pocketing $500. In many ways, this desire to "follow the job through" is a reflection of utter perversity, meaning that Angel Eyes could have simply rode away after being paid by and killing Stevens, leaving Baker to ponder his next move in pursuit of the stolen Confederate gold. But greed overtakes him, a compulsion that finally leads to his own violent death at the showdown in Sad Hill Cemetery, where after being shot a second time by Blondie, he tumbles into a convenient open grave with his Remington 1858 model revolver lying solitary and useless in the dirt.

Sergio Leone once remarked that Angel Eyes lacks a spirit, an integral part of the human subconscious mind that separates man from beast. Therefore, Angel Eyes is a brute without any redeeming values and symbolizes the antithesis of morality as a man lacking a soul. He could also be described as a tragic figure whose "fatal flaw" lies in his inability to feel emotion or express emotive gestures toward another person. In essence, Angel Eyes represents the worst of the "Best of the Bad" as a mercenary vulture, the "coldest killer in the West,"[8] a gunman with 200,000 reasons to kill.

FRANK TALBY: A MAN WITHOUT A CONSCIENCE

As a gunman, Frank Talby is a dying breed whose time has come and gone with the passing of the Old West into a civilized and peaceful place. By 1885, most of the Far West, beginning in California and extending into the Southwest and the Northern territories, had been transformed into a semblance of law and order with towns like Sacramento, Abilene, Kansas City, and even Tombstone, Arizona, under the lawful gun of a marshal and his deputies, hired to keep the peace and prevent outlaws and other ruffians from causing mayhem in the streets and the saloons. The average citizen who happened to call a town like Abilene home "had little sympathy for those who used guns in criminal activities" and did not generally care when a notorious gunman was killed. Although gunfights did occasionally erupt in the streets of these "nice, quiet little towns," most common folk felt that "those who lost their lives in gunfights needed shooting anyway" and deserved to be "run out of town and told never to return again"[9] or else face the town marshal with his Colt .45 drawn and ready for action.

This progress toward civilization eventually included the banning of firearms within city and town limits. On June 8, 1871, the *Abilene Chronicle* posted that the Chief of Police, none other than James Butler "Wild Bill" Hickok, wished to inform all citizens that carrying firearms in Abilene was illegal and that the law would be strictly enforced. "There's no bravery in carrying revolvers in a civilized community," declared the notice. "Such a practice is well enough and perhaps necessary when among Indians . . . but among white people it ought to be discontinued."[10] However, Hickok and his deputies continued to wear revolvers as symbols of their authority and as a warning to agitators that they were ready to use deadly force to keep order and maintain respectability.

This type of historical western landscape is all too familiar to Frank Talby, an intelligent and highly-skilled gunslinger without a conscience, much like Angel Eyes but far more calculating and cunning. Talby is also similar in some ways to Colonel Mortimer with his rather suave approach to solving problems and a natural talent for constructing devious plots and schemes. For Talby, all of these traits are shrewdly utilized in order to achieve his ultimate goal of controlling the small town of Clifton with the assistance of a somewhat dimwitted Scott Mary, the illegitimate son of a prostitute and the official town "garbage man" with big dreams of carrying his own Colt .45 someday which he believes will stop his superiors from calling him "a bastard" and an "ugly son of a bitch."

Upon arriving in Clifton one bright morning, Talby immediately begins his conquest of the town by befriending Scott Mary and initiating him into the lifestyle of a hedonist, a person who lives for pleasure and like Talby finds the local saloon comforting with its cheap whiskey and tables jutting into corners, the perfect place for conversation, drinking, and deception. But Talby's violent past as a gunslinger returns in the shape of Murph Allan Short, a worn-out old man and former sheriff who once ran Talby out of Abilene with a gun stuck in his back. At one point, Murph Allan mentions to Scott Mary that Talby is about forty-five years old, "a bad age for a gunman" when physical reflexes slow down and the body, after years of hard living, needs rest and relaxation. This is where Talby's primary motivation comes into play as a tired and aging gunfighter searching for a final place to call his own and to control as a tyrant. It is, in a sense, his final resting place, free from worry and responsibility where he can live out his days in relative peace and comfort.

One highly effective method which Talby utilizes as a way to control and manipulate the citizens of Clifton, especially the men involved in a ten year-old bank robbery scheme, is blackmail, a criminal act associated with some of the most villainous literary characters of all time. An excellent example is when Talby blackmails Abel Murray, the proprietor of the local saloon and a conspirator in the bank robbery scheme, by telling him he has proof of his involvement in the robbery. So as to retain his freedom, Murray signs a fake confession and turns all of his assets over to Talby, including the saloon which Talby burns to the ground after deciding to build his own drinking and gambling hall. Talby also uses emotional blackmail to win the confidence of Scott Mary; however, their relationship rapidly deteriorates when Scott realizes that Talby is nothing more than a conceited, ruthless killer with lots of blood on his hands.

Like Colonel Mortimer and Angel Eyes, Talby is adept in the use of firearms, ranging from an old flintlock rifle to his favorite weapon of choice, a Colt .45 revolver with two inches of barrel cut off and specially modified for "fanning" with the thumb. During his efforts to take control of Clifton, Talby kills at least a dozen men, such as the town barber, the head banker, the saloon owner, the town sheriff, several gunmen hired to kill him, and finally Murph Allan, Scott Mary's father figure and mentor whose death forces Scott to take up arms against Talby by using some of his own tried and true gunfighting lessons to defeat him in a tense showdown. With Talby lying wounded in the dirt, Scott Mary ponders one particular "Talbyism"—"If you wound a man, you'd better kill him or sooner or later, he's gonna kill you," and then proceeds to shoot Talby with a pistol that allegedly belonged to Doc Holliday, bringing an end to Talby's violent career as a professional gunslinger.

Like so many other villains, Frank Talby lacks the natural ability to balance out right from wrong which results in self-deception and a bloated view of his own importance. From an ethical standpoint, Talby, along with Angel Eyes, does not possess a conscience, an entity which Joseph D. Butler calls the "light within that when not darkened by self-deceit" acts as a guide for moral decisions and actions. When this entity is absent, it allows a human being to "act in any number of malicious or wicked ways without having any awareness" of the lack of morals.[11] Thus, in the end, Talby winds up as a victim of his own bloated ego, joining a long list of desperadoes, gunmen, and outlaws unable and unwilling to adapt to changing times.

ENDNOTES

1. McPherson, *Battle Cry of Freedom*, 435.
2. Ibid, 397.
3. Coco, Gregory A. *Confederates Killed in Action at Gettysburg.* Gettysburg, PA: Thomas Publications, 2001, 187.
4. *1st Sharpshooters South Carolina Volunteers.* National Civil War Association. Internet, 2010.
5. "Grand Horse Opera: The Best Westerns Celebrate Our History and Criticize the Ugly Stereotypes of the Genre." *American Scholar*, 77.3 (2008): 134.
6. Frayling, *Once Upon a Time in Italy: The Westerns of Sergio Leone.* New York: Harry N. Abrams, 2005, 108.
7. *Bad at the Bijou*, 51.
8. Locke, "Grand Horse Opera," 135.
9. Rosa, *The Gunfighter*, 61.
10. Ibid, 63.
11. *Fifteen Sermons Preached at the Rolls Chapel and a Dissertation on the Nature of Virtue.* London: G. Bell & Sons, Ltd., 1958, 158.

Fade Out: The Legacy of Lee Van Cleef

More than twenty years have come and gone since Lee Van Cleef rode out of town for the last time, leaving in the dust hundreds of dead men scattered about the vast landscapes of some of the best spaghetti westerns ever produced in Italy and shot in Spain during the middle to late 1960s. Of course, Van Cleef will be remembered for many years for his contributions to the Sergio Leone trilogy as Colonel Douglas Mortimer and Angel Eyes, but perhaps less so for his performances in a number of American and European westerns of varying degrees of quality, based on production, story, and the talents of the director.

It is not too difficult to imagine what other kinds of films Van Cleef might have made if he had lived longer or had found early and permanent success as a "heavy" in Hollywood before having to try his luck overseas in Italy. He once admitted that Leone had offered him the role of the sadistic Frank in *Once Upon a Time in the West* but turned it down because of its extreme depiction of violence against women and children. Leone supposedly also had plans to make a fourth "Man With No Name" film with Van Cleef, but Clint Eastwood decided not to participate and instead returned to Hollywood to direct and produce his own films under the banner of Malpaso.

Thus, Lee Van Cleef's legacy as an actor and as one of the best screen villains of the twentieth century is firmly established. However, it must be pointed out that his screen persona, at least as imaged in films where he plays the villain and the "bad guy," is diametrically opposed to his real personality; they are, in essence, complete opposites in just about every respect. To be more precise, the "badman" seen on the screen has virtually nothing in common with the real man, the real Lee Van Cleef. This is reminiscent of the late British horror film actor Sir Peter Cushing, described by many as "the gentle man of horror" and "Saint Peter" for his kindness and compassion, his devotion to his wife Helen, and his openness to friends, colleagues, and even complete strangers. Despite the obviousness of his admiration for the bottle and the enjoyment linked to drinking and carousing the bars of Los Angeles and other cities while in Europe shooting spaghetti westerns, Lee Van Cleef possessed some of the best human traits, such as a clear devotion to the happiness and well-being of his wife and children, and a sense of duty to his fellow man.

He was also capable of displaying genuine friendliness and was gifted when it came to interacting with others by listening to their dreams and desires, both on-screen and off, and a myriad of wild stories based on the exploits of some of Hollywood's most notorious western "heavies" like Neville Brand, Strother Martin, Luke Askew, and Jack Elam who longed for the old days when "the heavy was a heavy because he wanted money or the cattle, or he was just a plain son of a bitch!"[1]

In his autobiography *Them Ornery Mitchum Boys*, John Mitchum relates that circa 1960, Van Cleef "came to my house for lunch time to deliver (my) three-week-old baby girl" a special present, made up of perfume, baby powder, a mirror, and some hair brushes. Mitchum exalts his friend Lee for "the tenderness he displayed" which remained with him for many years, something that was "much more powerful than his screen image of filling cantankerous people full of holes."[2] Certainly, juxtaposing this tender reference against the brutality and villainy of Angel Eyes and Frank Talby draws up a collage of other traits which have probably never been considered by most readers, such as an ability to express great affection toward others and an easy-going attitude to take each day by itself; after all, as Van Cleef would probably agree, every day above ground is a good day.

In his foreword to this book, Mike Malloy mentions something that is of great importance to appreciating Lee Van Cleef the man and why his legacy continues to thrive some twenty years after his death. "Not a single one" of Van Cleef's co-stars whom Malloy had the chance to meet over the years, "had an outright negative thing to say" about him, a rather astounding statement considering that during the course of his professional career, Van Cleef interacted with hundreds of other actors, either on the set or outside of the mayhem that usually occurs when making a film.

Almost certainly, some of these interactions involved drinking, but it appears that Van Cleef, perhaps because of his experience and maturity, knew exactly what to say and when to say it, thus preserving his personal character. As a consequence of his good-natured approach to life and people, Van Cleef received much respect as a professional actor who took his career seriously. "I most often got the feeling that I was respected," he says, "and I got nothing but that. What went on behind my back, I'm not all that certain, but I got all the respect that any one man can handle."[3]

An additional personality trait is related to when Van Cleef refused to be filmed violently slapping that unfortunate prostitute in *The Good, The Bad, and The Ugly*. As an actor, Van Cleef had no qualms about film violence, but when it crossed the line into the realms of gratuitous cruelty and mistreatment, he would refuse to participate in scenes that included such human debasement. He once made it abundantly clear that beating women, abusing animals, and harming children was out of the question for him as a professional film performer. Also, Van Cleef felt that it was improper for a story to let the "bad guy" get away with his crime. "Let's not show the rapist or murderer," he once remarked, "getting away with it." Otherwise, if such a thing is allowed, "I don't want to be involved."[4]

If there is anything in Van Cleef's background that truly exemplifies his personality, it would be his courageous service in the US Navy during World War II while stationed aboard the USS *Incredible*. One particular event stands out like a giant advertisement billboard plastered with words like gutsy, brazen, stouthearted, chivalrous, fearless, and perhaps, foolhardy. This would be the time when Van Cleef, without first thinking about his own safety, jumped overboard to save little Rusty, the ship's mascot, from certain death in the cold December waters of the Mediterranean Sea. One could say this was the act of a nineteen year-old country bumpkin without a brain in his head; however, in reality, it symbolizes great courage, a selfless attitude, and a heartfelt concern for the lives of others, even if the other in this instance is a dog.

In the words of fellow actor and co-star Eli Wallach, Lee Van Cleef was "an excellent actor and an important contribution to the success of *The Good, The Bad, and The Ugly*. We became good friends during the filming. Lee was shy and his face was wonderfully alive, and we spent a lot of time together, particularly during the prisoner of war camp and the final shooting scenes in the cemetery. He left us much too soon."[5] Lee Van Cleef, a shy person? This is not so surprising, given the fact that many actors, even those considered as "heavies," are demure and unpretentious off-screen, almost to the point of timidity. But Van Cleef's shyness was certainly not reflected in his "wonderfully alive" face which will remain the penultimate image of the spaghetti western villain for decades to come.

* * * * * * * * *

Within the contrasting shadows of a dimly-lit saloon conveniently removed from the confines of reality, Lee Van Cleef, dressed in black from head to foot, sits pensively at a table with a bottle of whiskey and an ivory meerschaum pipe dangling from his lips. His hawk-like eyes move furtively around the room, always cautious of approaching danger in the shape of a young gunslinger out to make a name for himself. The saloon doors suddenly creak open, filling the atmosphere with dusty light and apprehension. Van Cleef slowly reaches for his holstered Colt Navy revolver and draws the hammer back until it clicks, ready to fire.

As expected, a young man with a Colt .45 stuck in his waistband stands in the open saloon doorway. He steps cautiously, knowing that one wrong move could send him dead to the floor with a bullet in his heart, but he presses on until Van Cleef motions for him to sit in an empty chair at the table.

"Are you Lee Van Cleef?" asks the young man as a bead of sweat rolls down his face.

"Who else would I be?"

"I've heard you're a cold-hearted, mean son of a bitch, a really bad man."

"What else have you heard, boy?"

"That you've killed a hundred men without blinking an eye."

Van Cleef smiles wickedly and leans in close to the young man, close enough to smell the odor of alcohol on his breath.

"Just stand up," he says, "and get the hell outta here."

"I've also heard," replies the young man, "that you like beating women, an' kicking dogs. I guess you really are nuthin' but a coward."

The wicked smile fades away and is replaced by a cold stare, not of anger, but of dishonor.

"So you've heard I've killed a hundred men without blinking an eye, right? You're wrong, boy. I've killed one hundred and one men."

The young man's face goes expressionless, and in an instant, Van Cleef's Colt Navy revolver explodes, and the young man and his chair flies backwards and hard against the wall. Van Cleef stands up, pours a shot of whiskey, and throws it back in one gulp. He looks down at the young man, now with blood oozing through his shirt and his Colt .45 still in his waistband.

"Just remember, boy," says Van Cleef. "Never trust anyone."

The young man smiles, then his head tips dead to one side. Van Cleef lights his pipe and casually heads for the saloon doors. As he exits, he turns and smiles wickedly once again.

"I am the best of the bad," he says, "and don't you forget it."

ENDNOTES

1. Horner, *Bad at the Bijou*, 19.
2. Pacifica, CA: Creatures at Large Press, 1988, 180.
3. Horner, 55.
4. Ibid, 57.
5. Handwritten letter to Christopher Gullo, October 20, 2003

BIBLIOGRAPHY

1st Sharpshooters South Carolina Volunteers. National Civil War Association. 2010. http://www.ncwa.org/index.php?option=com_content&task=view&id=56&Itemid=57.

"Actor Lee Van Cleef, 64; Played Villains." Associated Press Release obit. December 18, 1989.

Beveridge, Allan and Graeme Yorston. "I Drink, Therefore I Am: Alcohol and Creativity." *Journal of the Royal Society of Medicine*, 92 (1999): 646-648.

Blum, Daniel. A *Pictorial History of the American Theatre, 1900 to 1951*. New York: Greenberg Publishers, 1951.

Butler, Joseph D. *Fifteen Sermons Preached at the Rolls Chapel and a Dissertation on the Nature of Virtue*. London: G. Bell & Sons, Ltd., 1958.

Chinn, Stephen, Kenneth Thomas, and the Kansas Heritage Group. *Kansas Gunfighters*. 2010. http://www.vlib.us/old_west/guns.html.

Coco, Gregory A. *Confederates Killed in Action at Gettysburg*. Gettysburg, PA: Thomas Publications, 2001.

Cumbow, Robert C. *The Films of Sergio Leone*. New York: Rowman & Littlefield, 2008.

Edwards, Daniel. *Sergio Leone.* 2002. http://archive.sensesofcinema.com/contents/directors/02/leone.html.

Edwards, William B. *Civil War Guns.* Secaucus, NJ: Castle Books, 1982.

Eliot, Marc. *American Rebel: The Life of Clint Eastwood.* New York: Harmony Books, 2009.

Frayling, Christopher. *Once Upon a Time in Italy: The Westerns of Sergio Leone.* New York: Harry N. Abrams, Inc., 2005.

Freud, Sigmund. *New Introductory Lectures on Psychoanalysis.* New York: W.W. Norton, 1995.

Horner, William R. *Bad at the Bijou.* Jefferson, NC: McFarland & Company, 1982.

Internet Movie Database (IMDB). 2010. http://www.imdb.com.

Interview with Mike Malloy. *Lee Van Cleef Forum.* November 7, 2009. www.chezleevancleef.com.

Jung, Carl. "Archetypes and the Collective Unconscious." *The Collected Works of C.G. Jung.* Vol. 9. New York: Princeton University Press, 1977.

Kiral, Cenk. *The Good, The Bad, and Luciano Vincenzoni.* 1998. http://www.fistful-of-leone.com/articles/vince.html.

Knowles, George. *Charles Godfrey Leland* (1824-1903). 2001. http://www.controverscial.com/Charles%20Godfrey%20Leland.htm.

LaFeber, Walter. *The New Empire: An Interpretation of American Expansion, 1860-1898.* Ithaca, NY: Cornell University Press, 1998.

"Lee Van Cleef Returns to TV, Villainous Appearance Intact." *Montreal Gazette*. June 6, 1977, p. 34.

"Lee Van Cleef Seriously Hurt." *Somerville Gazette*. October 16, 1958.

Leonard, Elmore, and Louis L'Amour. *Western Movies: Classic Wild West Films*. UK: Severn House, Ltd., 1997.

Lewis, John. *American Film: A History.* New York: W.W. Norton & Company, 2007.

Locke, Richard. "Grand Horse Opera: The Best Westerns Celebrate Our History and Criticize the Ugly Stereotypes of the Genre." *American Scholar*, 77.3 (2008): 130-136.

Malloy, Mike. *Lee Van Cleef: A Biographical, Film and Television Reference*. Jefferson, NC: McFarland & Company, 2005.

McPherson, James M. *Battle Cry of Freedom: The Civil War Era*. New York: Oxford University Press, 1998.

Mitchum, John. *Them Ornery Mitchum Boys*. Pacifica, CA: Creatures at Large Press, 1988.

Nolan, Frederick. *Wild West: History, Myth, and the Making of America*. Secaucus, NJ: Chartwell Books, 2004.

Pingenot, Benjamin E. *Charles Angelo Siringo*. The Handbook of Texas Online. 2010. http://www.tshaonline.org/handbook/online/articles/SS/fsi32.html.

Rosa, Joseph G. *The Gunfighter: Man or Myth?* Oklahoma City: University of Oklahoma Press, 1969.

"Sailor Dives Off Ship to Save Pup Washed into Sea." *Somerville Gazette*. December 17, 1944.

Scott, Tony. "How the Western Was Won." *New York Times Magazine*. 2007, 54.

Sergio Leone on Lee Van Cleef. Spaghetti Cinema. May 4, 2009. http://wconnolly. Blogspot.com/2009/05/sergio-leone-on-lee-van-cleef.html.

Shaplin, Adriano. *The Tragedy of Thomas Hobbes*. New York: Oberon Books, 2009.

Shillingberg, William B. "Wyatt Earp and the 'Buntline Special' Myth." Kansas *Historical Quarterly*. Vol. 42 no. 2 (1976): 113-154.

Spaghetti Western Database. 2010. http://www.spaghetti-western.net/index.php/Main_Page.

USS Incredible (AM-249). *Department of the Navy—Naval Historical Center*. 1999. http://www.history.navy.mil/photos/sh-usn/usnsh-i/am249.htm.

USS SC-681—Submarine Chaser of the SC-497 Class. 2010. http://www.uboat.net/allies/warships/ship/8898.html.

Voytilla, Stuart and Christopher Vogler. *Myth and the Movies: Discovering the Mythic Structure*. Studio City, CA: Michael Wiese Books, 1999.

Wallach, Eli. *The Good, The Bad, and Me*. Harcourt & Company, 2005.

Wilson, Earl. "Van Cleef Works at Keeping His 'Mean SOB' Reputation." *Sarasota Herald Tribune*. January 31, 1978. p. 12-A.

INDEX

A Fistful of Dollars 35
A Pistol for Ringo 8
Alvin Theatre 19
Bad Man's River 27
Betts, Tom 11
Beyond the Law 3, 27
"Buntline Special" 51-52
Captain Apache 27
Colt, Samuel 41
Colt .45 "Peacemaker" revolver 49, 50-51
Colt 1851 Navy revolver 49, 52, 53
Corman, Roger 6
Cushing, Sir Peter 72
Day of Anger 3, 8, 11, 27, 34, 36, 37
Death Rides a Horse 3, 8, 27
Django 8
Eastwood, Clint 7, 9, 27, 34
For a Few Dollars More 2, 7, 8, 10,11, 25, 34, 36, 37
Fonda, Henry 7
God's Gun 27
Heaven Can Wait 19
High Noon 10, 20-21
High Plains Drifter 34
Horner, William R. 19
How the West Was Won 24
Il terrore dell'Oklahoma ("The Terror of Oklahoma") 43
It Conquered the World 6
Judson, E.C.Z. (Ned Buntline) 40, 41

Jung, Carl 37
Kiral, Cenk 11
La sceriffa ("The Sheriff was a Lady") 43
Leland, Charles Godfrey 14
Leone, Sergio 7, 9, 23, 24, 25, 26, 53
Malloy, Mike 11, 72
Mister Roberts 20
Mitchum, John 24, 72
Morris, Maynard 19
Once Upon a Time in the West 8, 71
Our Town 19
Pale Rider 34
Remington 1858 New Army .44 revolver 49, 50, 52
Return of Sabata 27
Ride Lonesome 23, 43
Rosa, Joseph G. 42, 44
Sabata 27
Samuel Colt Company 50
Shane 33, 48
Siringo, Charlie 44-45
The Bounty Hunter 45
The Big Gundown 3, 8
The Bravados 21
The Conqueror 29
The Good, The Bad, and The Ugly 3, 9, 10, 11, 24, 27, 34, 35, 36, 37, 49
The Grand Duel 3, 27
The Great Train Robbery 43
The Man Who Shot Liberty Valance 24

The Stranger and the Gunfighter 27
Tierra Brutal ("The Savage Guns") 44
Uberti, Aldo 53
Van Cleef, Lee:
    Auto accident 22
    Boy Scouts 14
    Clinton Music Hall Players 19
    Death and burial 28-29
    Drinking 21-24

Method acting 20
Somerville, NJ., childhood & youth 14
United States Navy 15-18
Van Cleef, Clarence Leroy Sr. (his father) 15
Van Cleef, Patsy Ruth (1st wife) 18
Van Fleet, Marion (his mother) 14
Vincenzoni, Luciano 23, 25
Wallach, Eli 20, 74

www.ingramcontent.com/pod-product-compliance
Lightning Source LLC
Chambersburg PA
CBHW070938160426
43193CB00011B/1728